United Nations.

ECONOMIC COMMISSION FOR EUROPE
Geneva

Committe on Water Problems.

Systems of water statistics in the ECE region

*A report prepared under the auspices
of the ECE Committee on Water Problems*

UNITED NATIONS
New York, 1986

NOTE

Symbols of United Nations documents are composed of capital letters combined with figures. Mention of such a symbol indicates a reference to a United Nations document.

The designations employed and the presentation of the material in this publication do not imply the expression of any opinion whatsoever on the part of the Secretariat of the United Nations concerning the legal status of any country, territory, city or area or of its authorities, or concerning the delimitation of its frontiers or boundaries.

ECE/WATER/43

UNITED NATIONS PUBLICATION

Sales No. E.86.II.E.22

ISBN 92-1-116373-0

01500P

CONTENTS

PREFACE

Since its inception, the Committee on Water Problems has paid particular attention to the development and application of water-use statistics, with a view to identifying problems and exploring possibilities to promote the rational use of water in the ECE region.

In a first attempt, the Committee, at its fifth session, endorsed a system of statistics applied in reviewing water use in ECE countries (WATER/R.19). A similar approach was applied to data collection during preparation of the ECE regional report to the United Nations Water Conference in Mar del Plata (Argentina) in 1977 (E/CONF.70/6). Another application of a somewhat modified system of water-use statistics can be found in the ECE report on Long-term Perspectives for Water Use and Supply in the ECE Region (ECE/WATER/26). In that report, statistical information on water-resources demand and use had been combined to show water-management balances (see also ECE/WATER/5). An expanded system of statistics was applied to the preparation of the report on Purification of Domestic Sewage and Industrial Waste Water (ECE/WATER/36).

With regard to ambient water quality statistics, the Committee has studied methods for defining standards of water quality. The report on this exercise contains a set of principles for the establishment of quality criteria and classification of surface waters along with suggestion for a uniform presentation of the results for statistical purposes (WATER/R.84 and Addendum 1).

The Committee on Water Problems, at its thirteenth session in 1981, launched specific activities with a view to examining ways and means of making components of national water statistics directly comparable, in particular with regard to: the availability of water resources and off-stream water uses (both in terms of water quantity and quality) as well as prevention and control of water pollution. Implementation of these activities has followed four action lines:

- Carrying out surveys of national systems of water-use statistics and ambient water quality statistics in ECE countries;

- Co-sponsoring the development of a draft standard international classification of water use and water quality together with the Conference of European Statisticians;

- Designing a system of water-use statistics, and

- Compiling definitions of terms used in the system of water-use statistics and in the draft standard international classification.

SURVEYS OF NATIONAL STATISTICAL SYSTEMS

In analysing systems of water statistics in ECE countries, the Committee on Water Problems distinguished among four basic categories:

- in situ (ambient) water quality   - off-stream water quality

- in situ water quantity (hydrology)   - off-stream water quantity

Quality and quantity aspects relate to both surface water and ground water and to their uses and management.

The Committee surveyed national systems of water-use statistics in ECE countries. This was done in order to examine approaches allowing for the collection of data on quantity and quality of off-stream water uses, including abstraction, make-up, distribution, losses, consumption, reuse, recycling, treatment and discharge.

At the same time the Committee carried out the survey on national systems of ambient water-quality statistics in ECE countries. This was undertaken in order to compare methods of national statistics reflecting water quality in rivers, lakes, reservoirs and aquifers. The survey concentrated on ambient water-quality statistics covering in situ water uses that are dependent on water quality. Not dealt with are statistical systems for hydrology - an area already well-developed in many countries - nor related in situ uses such as navigation, timber-floating or hydroelectric power production.

The information should be considered as complementary to the report on water-quality monitoring, prepared under the auspices of the Committee. Water-quality monitoring and statistics are closely related: comprehensive, well-founded statistical systems are a prerequisite to efficient monitoring of quality; monitoring programmes constitute the main data source for statistics on ambient water-quality.

Information in this survey has been drawn from various sources, in particular government contributions to activities carried out under the auspices of the Committee on Water Problems (CWP), the Senior Advisers to ECE Governments on Environmental Problems (SAEP) and the Conference of European Statisticians (CES). A detailed list follows:

- Survey of national statistics regarding water use and water quality (CWP, 1982-1984);

- Ad hoc Meeting on Environmental Indicators (CES, 1984);

- Informal meeting on Water Use and Quality Statistics (CES, 1983);

- Informal meeting on General Methodological Problems in Environmental Statistics (CES, 1983);

- Ad hoc Meeting on Statistics of Water Use and Quality (CWP/CES, 1982);

- Comparison and analysis of methods for defining standards of water quality (CWP, 1977-1981);

- Informal meeting on framework for environmental statistics (SAEP/CES, 1981);

- Seminar on Environmental Statistics, held in Warsaw, Poland (SAEP/CES, 1980);

- Ad hoc meeting on Environmental Statistics (SAEP/CES, 1978);

- Survey on national work in the field of environmental statistics (CES, 1976-1977).

Apart from governmental contributions, including country monographs, seminar discussion papers and replies to questionnaires, national yearbooks were also consulted. Both surveys were released for general distribution by the Committee on Water Problems (seventeenth session, November 1985).

DRAFT STANDARD INTERNATIONAL CLASSIFICATION

Following an invitation extended by the Conference of European Statisticians at its twenty-eighth session (June 1980), the Committee decided to co-operate with the Conference of European Statisticians in the development of a draft standard international classification of water use and quality. To this end, both Principal Subsidiary Bodies convened jointly ad hoc meetings in May 1981, January 1982 and January 1985. The draft standard international classification was elaborated by the ad hoc Meeting on Statistics of Water Use and Quality convened in 1982 (WATER/AC.5/2/Annex I) and supplemented and amended at the meeting convened in 1985 (WATER/AC.5/4).

Already in 1982, the Group of Experts on Aspects of Water Quality and Quantity, at its tenth session, had stated that the draft classification, when further developed, could constitute a valuable reference document and thus might provide guidance in the elaboration of a system of international water statistics. In 1985, the Conference of European Statisticans and the Committee on Water Problems took note of the draft ECE Standard International Classification of Water Use and Quality in its revised form. Both Principal Subsidiary Bodies approved also the results (WATER/AC.5/4) of the ad hoc meeting convened in January 1985.

SYSTEM OF WATER-USE STATISTICS

The Committee on Water Problems, at its fifteenth session, decided to elaborate a system of water-use statistics, in co-operation with the Conference of European Statisticians. The system would be in line with activities carried out under the auspices of the Committee. The objective was to facilitate the best possible presentation of all national statistical data so as to enhance their comparability, both with regard to water quality and quantity. Taking into account comments and remarks made by the Group of Experts on Aspects of Water Quality as well as those of the 1985 ad hoc Meeting on Statistics of Water Use and Quality, the Committee finalized work on the system of water-use statistics at its seventeenth session in 1985.

It should be underlined that the ad hoc Meeting had noted with satisfaction that the draft system and the draft classification were fully integrated and that there was no duplication. Parallel to the work on the draft classification and the draft system, categories and terms used in both drafts have been described and defined, inter alia, on the basis of various glossaries prepared within the framework of previous studies, or under the auspices of other organizations. Among the most important sources were the following:

- Index of essential terms used in the manual for the compilation of balances of water resources and needs (ECE/WATER/5, appendix B);

- Terminology on economic incentives in water supply and waste water disposal systems, including the fixing of charges (ECE/WATER/16);

- Explanatory notes to the ad hoc questionnaire on techniques and means
  for the purification of industrial and municipal sewage effluents, as
  adopted by the Committee on Water Problems at its twelfth session
  (ECE/WATER/25);

- Terminology used in the report on long-term perspectives for water use
  and supply in the ECE region (ECE/WATER/26);

- Description of terms and categories used in the ECE draft standard
  international classification of water use and quality (WATER/AC.5/2);

- Water Quality - Vocabulary - Parts 1 to 5 elaborated by the
  International Organization for Standardization (ISO).

Taking into account relevant modifications and amendments suggested by
the ad hoc Meeting in January 1985, a full set of definitions of terms for use
in systems of water statistics was adopted by the Conference of European
Statisticians and the Committee on Water Problems at their respective sessions
in 1985. It should be noted in this respect that the terms appearing in both
the draft classification and the draft system are defined identically.

*   *   *

The results of this work on water statistics are used in the present
activities of both Principal Subsidiary Bodies:

- The Committee on Water Problems has taken the uniform system of
  water-use statistics as a basis for collection of data for the Survey
  on Current Trends and Policies and Future Prospects regarding the Use
  of Water Resources and Water Pollution Control, carried out in the
  years 1986 and 1987.

- The Conference of European Statisticians applies the draft standard
  international classification of water use and quality and the set of
  definitions of terms related to systems of water statistics when
  compiling the water section of the experimental compendium of ECE
  environment statistics.

The Committee on Water Problems, at its seventeenth session endorsed the
present report for publication. It should be noted that the information
contained in this study, particularly in the surveys, reflects the situation
prevailing in November 1985. In accordance with established practice, this
document is published under the sole responsibility of the secretariat.

INTRODUCTION

In all ECE countries it has long been understood that knowledge of
water's availability and its physical behaviour was vital to the development
of national water resources. It is not unusual to have time-series dating
back as far as the nineteenth century, especially concerning surface run-off,
water levels of both surface and ground water, measurements of precipitation,
evaporation and temperature. National hydrological offices have been
systematically improving their data collection, processing and publication of
information on a routine basis; thus, hydrographical services in all
countries constitute a well co-ordinated, efficiently structured mechanism for
exploring quantities in the hydrological cycle. They provide, inter alia,
data for flood and drought management, for regulating water courses and for
some in situ uses of the resource (navigation, hydropower production or
timber-floating).

Regular measurement of the quality of water resources, particularly the
recording of quantity and quality data on water use started in a few countries
some 20 years ago, while in other countries water-use and quality statistics
may either not yet exist, or be under development, or have only an episodic,
sectorial character. With ever-increasing water shortages, and in view of the
threat of water pollution, however, Governments are searching for principles
of rational water use. The principles accompany a shift in policies towards
water-demand and water-use management. Hence the need to develop water-use
and water quality statistics that are expanded in scope, more systematic and
rendered comparable on a national if not an international level. For modern
and future-oriented water management, regular water-quality surveys and
water-use investigations are essential as they provide the background data and
basic information.

Information that identifies water pollution problems, changing
water-quality trends and new water-use patterns in all sectors of the national
economy is invaluable. It enables an assessment to be made of the
effectiveness of regulatory measures and economic instruments in achieving the
desired level of water use, consumption, reuse and recycling, and reveals
their impact on water quality. It further provides a basis for revising,
where necessary, the instruments applied in water management and control. In
river basins where water-use projects are many and varied, synchronization of
operations is essential in order to make the best use of water or to minimize
pollution. Here again, adequate reliable data are the key to operational
efficiency.

In most countries, policy-makers and decision-makers in water management,
and more particularly in water quality control, have become aware of the need
for comprehensive quality statistics covering most water bodies, either for
surface or underground waters, extending over long periods of time.
Statistics have particular relevance for determining actual or potential
impacts of human activities on the aquatic environment, and identifying
quality changes in ambient water over time as well as their effects on ecology
and the economy.

Comparable systems of water-quality statistics are essential in assessing
the need for, or the effectiveness of, policies designed to prevent or reverse
deterioration of the aquatic environment. Water authorities are not the only
users of such statistics. Data are also of great importance for industry,

agriculture and the public at large, for a better understanding of
water-quality control policies and in order to evaluate external costs and
benefits accruing from measures dealing with production and consumption
activities. Well-founded statistical data-series thus have far-reaching
applications.

An active and future-oriented water management policy must be formulated
on the basis of consolidated statistical information. For this it is
indispensable to render existing statistical systems for water-supply and
water-quality data more efficient and more meaningful. Moreover data must be
comparable, as far as possible, both on a national and on an international
level. Emphasis must be given to drawing up inventories of the fate of
noxious substances in the aquatic environment, systematic investigations of
their sources, their synergistic and cumulative effects and their impact on
humanity and the environment. Increased attention will have to be paid to the
development of an improved data base regarding water use, including
abstraction, use and reuse, as well as treatment and discharge from both a
quantitative and qualitative point of view. Such disaggregated data-sets are
considered fundamental in pursuing and promoting rational water use in all
economic sectors. The uniform system of water-use statistics presented in
Part One may serve as a guide to developing water-use data sets.

The review of country reports shows that water management authorities in
various ECE countries are questioning whether existing water statistics do, in
fact, respond to the present demands of pollution control and rational use of
water. A great deal of work has already been done in the search for
improvement of statistical systems still in use or for more advanced
techniques by which to replace them. The recent exchange of experience gained
on a national level, which was promoted by the Committee on Water Problems in
co-operation with the Conference of European Statisticians, was intended to
facilitate the formulation, application and improvement of ambient
water-quality statistics and water-use statistics in ECE member countries.
When amending or changing existing statistical systems, the opportunity may be
taken to strive for uniformity of future systems and to smooth out as much as
possible (and as much as local circumstances permit) the conceptual anomalies
and technical differences in existing systems.

The Committee on Water Problems, in close co-operation with the
Conference of European Statisticians, has undertaken surveys of statistics on
water quality and water use. These surveys, carried out over three years,
entailed a review of the present situation and the outlook regarding relevant
national systems of water statistics. The surveys drew upon information
provided by the following ECE Governments: Austria, Belgium, Bulgaria,
Byelorussian SSR, Canada, Czechoslovakia, Denmark, Finland, France, German
Democratic Republic, Germany, Federal Republic of, Greece, Hungary, Italy,
Netherlands, Norway, Poland, Portugal, Spain, Sweden, Switzerland,
Ukrainian SSR, USSR, United Kingdom, and United States of america. Relevant
work undertaken under the auspices of the Council for Mutual Economic
Assistance (CMEA) and the European Economic Community (EEC) was also reflected.

A compilation of the surveys is contained in Part B of the present report.

Conclusions drawn by the Committee from the two surveys are set out in
Part A together with the uniform system of water-use statistics comprising
data sets recommended by the Committee as essential statistical information.
The terms used in statistical systems are also defined.

PART A: CONCLUSIONS AND RECOMMENDATIONS

I.   THE SIGNIFICANCE OF STATISTICS FOR INTEGRATED WATER MANAGEMENT AND THEIR
     MAIN CHARACTERISTICS

From the findings presented and the experience now gained in various
countries, it is becoming evident that increasing significance is being
attached to the development of water statistics or the adaptation of those
already existing to the greater exigencies of water management. This general
trend is echoed in the ECE Declaration of Policy on the Rational Use of Water
whereby ECE member Governments undertook

> "to increase their efforts to develop or improve methods for the regular
> collection, the proper analysis and the timely dissemination of directly
> comparable data on water abstraction, use, consumption and discharge,
> both in terms of quantity and quality, in the various economic sectors.
> These statistics on water use and water quality should be considered
> along with existing data of available water resources to help to identify
> water-deficient areas, and those vulnerable and sensitive to future water
> shortages as well as to foresee possible conflicts between water users.
> These statistics should also be used in the evaluation of effects of
> administrative and economic components of long-term strategies. In this
> respect, relevant experience and information gained in the implementation
> of water-management measures should be considered an important input in
> water management planning."

Society has a collective interest in wisely managing its water
resources. Precise information on the actual state of, and anticipated
changes in, quantity and quality of these resources is essential. Adequate
information is fundamental to public understanding and support for unpopular
measures taken to promote rational use of water and to control pollution.
Information on determinants of water use and water quality and the effect of
changes on water use is equally vital. If control of water use by influencing
water demand is seen as a management tool then statistical information as to
the determinants of demand, supply, use and discharge as well as their
interrelationship takes on added significance. Moreover, capital-intensive
water management systems require a long lead time for planning and design;
once constructed, they need to be integrated into the existing system and
operated efficiently. It is thus most desirable for water management to
describe the relevant determinants by means of appropriate statistical
information and to detect in advance any changes in their complex
interrelationships. By reducing errors in the design of projects and in other
investment and allocation decisions, the statistical information so derived
would facilitate efficient, least-cost management of water resources.

A major aim is to produce the right kind of data for improving the
formulation, implementation and evaluation of water policies. For purposes of
strategic planning, resource allocation, water-demand management and pollution
control, water statistics should allow for analyses of alternative courses of
action satisfying alternative sets of socio-economic and environmental goals.

Water statistics could support and strengthen the water component in a
country's sectorial policies. Often sectorial policies have significant
implications for water resources, both in terms of quantity and quality. As
such, they may be in direct conflict with the stated aim of specific national

water policies if efficient co-ordination among the various sectors is not guaranteed and if the water component is not integrated into these policies. Accurate water statistics are needed also regarding trends and their potential impact on water resources. Many situations could be postulated in which such information is essential, for example, in relation to agricultural policies encouraging intensification both through financial support for modernization schemes and pricing policy. Intensification of agriculture has a number of consequences for the aquatic environment: drainage of wetlands, increased water abstraction for irrigation, increased use of chemicals, application of manure and consequent pollution; point and non-point sources of pollution to both surface water and ground water.

The aim of obtaining water statistics and time series is to develop balanced policies which provide, together with development strategies in specific economic sectors, efficient measures to promote the rational use of water. They are a valuable tool in the protection of water resources against pollution and over-exploitation before water resources are irreversibly damaged or to take steps to apply remedial measures if damage has occurred.

Another purpose of an information system on water use and water quality is to indicate which sectors of water management need further research and where financial support and scientific efforts should be directed. Possible sectors include those where: (a) ground water pollution is most severe and thus research is needed to identify causes, ascertain rates of change and design possible measures both of a protective and remedial nature; (b) suitable control sites exist for base-line studies against which to assess human-induced changes on the aquatic environment; (c) actual and potential conflicts between various water users have been reported and thus where detailed studies are necessary in order to shed light on their specific impacts on water resources and to monitor changes owing to protection and to apply demand-oriented measures; (d) vulnerable resources exist which might need careful monitoring, surveillance and studies to guard against increasing environmental stress; and (e) methodological research is necessary to improve current monitoring techniques and data evaluation procedures.

For a statistical system to be both effective and acceptable, it should satisfy a number of criteria, including, among others, the need for consistency of results; flexibility; transparency and scientific rigour in the methodology; cost-effectiveness in its implementation; centralization and structuring; integration and co-ordination; as well as the need for compatibility on an international level.

NEED FOR CONSISTENCY, FLEXIBILITY AND TRANSPARENCY

In any information system consistency is essential. It may be achieved in various ways. Results should be regionally and nationally consistent in that they produce similar answers for similar situations. They should also be consistent over time, so that trends in water statistics are neither hidden nor distorted and time series yield meaningful results. Additionally, the results should be consistent between operators: the prejudices or personal bias of individual operators should not affect the statistics provided by the system. Likewise, data collection should be designed in such a way that the subjectivity of respondents is reduced to a minimum. These requirements can only be met if, above all, the information system is reasonably objective and value-free. Any value judgements involved must be made explicitly and according to defined criteria. Moreover, they should not affect the basic data. Consistency requires also that the system not have any in-built regional or local biases (e.g. towards agricultural areas). Instead, it should be sensitive to the full range of water-related conditions found in a country.

Related to the need for consistency is the requirement of flexibility. As noted, the statistical system should be able to cope with a wide range of problems in integrated water management at various levels (local, regional, national international). It will also need to deal with a considerable range of data from other economic sectors. Moreover, with time it is likely that the demands upon the information system will alter as new problems become apparent, as new sources of data emerge, as socio-political priorities change and as scientific knowledge and technical skill develop. If the information system is to be spared imminent obsolescence, it should be kept flexible enough to adjust to changing demands and circumstances.

Flexibility can best be achieved by ensuring that data are stored in their raw form, with a high degree of disaggregation. Versatility is also aided by a system which has the capacity to be discrete or modular in structure, so that individual components can be modified without detriment to other parts of the system. It is also essential that the data requirements be reasonably flexible, so that the method is not hampered by problems of data availability.

Water managers working with water statistics and experts using statistical data often find that the level of aggregation or reported unit of observation is not well suited to the majority of problems at hand. Sometimes information is in a form that makes it difficult to synthesize water data with ancillary data available at a different level of aggregation or unit of observation. This may happen when water data are collected according to statistical systems which do not take into account the subsequent use of data in water management. Water statistics should not be drawn up simply for the sake of statisticians but must respond to the various exigencies arising from water policies, their formulation, adaptation, and implementation. An appropriate level of aggregation can distort the subsequent analytical work and limit the inferential utility of the data. Unnecessary resolution on the other hand only increases costs in operating the system. A fair balance should therefore be struck as to the most appropriate level of disaggregation.

In order to ensure that results are consistent, that the method can be adapted as required and that non-experts in water statistics can appreciate the results, it is important that the information system be based on an explicit, clear structure. Thereby it will be possible to check results more readily, see how results were derived and thus justify any conclusions or observations for the actual users of the system. This aim is all the more important because of the complexity of problems in integrated water management and the variety of scales on which the system may be applied. Errors or misunderstandings at the level of data collection, processing or analysis may feed into decisions if the internal functioning of the system is not immediately apparent, verifiable and validated as necessary. This only underlines the need for a system in which any value judgement or subjective determination is minimized and where any guesswork necessary is so defined. The system should also contain the facility for presenting results in a wide variety of ways and through appropriate media.

Many existing water-use and water-quality data are not actual measurements but rather estimates provided in response to a questionnaire or survey. Especially in the case of self-supply there is an incentive to report a rate of water use or a degree of pollution discharged which coincides exactly with the terms of permits for abstraction and discharge. The methods used to extrapolate the estimate on the basis of a sample should therefore be described in detail so that the estimate can be verified. This also holds true for water-use and water-quality data evaluated by indirect methods based on production figures, manpower or other indicators gleaned from manufacturing enterprises, agricultural activities and population censuses.

Adequate and comprehensible definitions of terms used in the statistical system, their units, territorial repartition and time coverage, abbreviations and symbols applied, averages or extrema, etc. should be provided with a view to avoiding ambiguities. This would facilitate implementation of such systems and the analysis of data gained. Descriptions should be furnished of the methodologies used in order to enable the users of data from statistical systems to assess the value of the information in terms of the method applied in collecting and processing it. Indeed, adequate interpretation of data on water use and quality is often impossible without sufficient knowledge of the methodology. This is particularly so for sections of the system dealing with water-quality variables. For the envisaged ecosystems approach, new statistical indicators need to be developed in order to describe with sufficient scientific rigour the complex interrelationship of specific aquatic ecosystems and their changes. For this the statistical system will have to be consistent in its use of terms, concepts and definitions. As stated by the Group of Experts on Aspects of Water Quality and Quantity at its tenth session, the draft standard international classification of water use and quality could constitute a valuable reference document. It would thus offer guidance in the elaboration of suitable systems or the adaptation of existing ones.

NEED FOR COST-EFFECTIVENESS

If the information system is to be viable, it must satisfy certain cost constraints. While this requirement imposes limits it also presents challenges regarding efficiency of such systems. The major implication concerns data needed for water-use and water-quality statistics. In order to reduce costs, often the data being used in the system are those which are already available or which can be collected relatively cheaply and rapidly. Such data, however, may vary considerably in quality, resolution and form. Consequently, information systems may be reduced to the level of the lowest common denominator, that is limited by the quality of the least satisfactory information, the most gross level of aggregation or only those features for which particular types of data are nationally or regionally available. It is therefore often not opportune to spare resources on the data collection side as, in the long run, it will be necessary to collect primary data on water use and water quality, although every effort should be made to avoid duplication.

Data needs should be kept to a minimum that is compatible with the functions of the system. This should be clearly determined in advance. The benefits of the system will be optimized with multiple use of the statistical information. This means that information should be made available in a form as intelligible and useful to as many users as possible, including the general public. Everyone concerned needs to be continuously aware of the state of the aquatic environment and the changes of water-use patterns and their impacts on water resources.

A statistical system will be rendered more efficient as experience is gained with its implementation. Thus there is a need to monitor its operation and to change the procedures where appropriate. Economic theory tells us that, if the net benefits from data collection are to be maximized, data should be collected up to that point where the increase in benefits attributable to additional data is just equal to the incremental cost of procuring that data. Such a cost-benefit balance may sometimes seem elusive. Furthermore, it may be difficult to estimate the economic benefits attributable to data collection.

NEED FOR CENTRALIZATION AND STRUCTURING

As water-use data are often scattered among water agencies at the local, regional, State or federal levels, not to mention various water users, it becomes difficult to identify the extent of the existing data. Indeed, one of the major problems in water statistics could be that there is no central repository or cataloguing office for data. Such an office might also lessen the cost of data procurement by lowering search costs and redundant data collection efforts. Water-use and water-quality data comprise a public good such that one use of the data does not preclude other simultaneous or subsequent use. Least-cost dissemination of water-related information, and thus maximization of net benefits from the data, probably requires a central repository or cataloguing office. Such an agency might also identify existing and scattered water statistics and assess their utility in the context of a given system.

With respect to the foregoing, in particular the need for cost-effectiveness, it becomes apparent that an information system could usefully be structured on the national level as a framework system for the collection, retrieval and presentation of essential data on water use and water quality. Time-series on key indicators could thus be developed. Surveys dealing with specific managerial questions and data collection of a more disaggregated nature could then be integrated into the framework where needed and complement it in a co-ordinated manner. For detailed decisions (e.g. about the impact of local projects) precise and specific information would be required although this may be useful only at the project-formulation level and at analysis stages.

What is needed for the national or regional level is a system of universal character which might: (a) act as a mechanism to identify those areas or problems in the field of water management needing urgent measures for rational use of water and control of pollution; (b) provide competent water authorities with development trends in water management for comprehensive planning on a national level; (c) provide information about the quality and use of water resources to regional water authorities who are planning local developments, or those in neighbouring or similar areas; and (d) reduce the costs of water-management planning by revealing early in the planning stage the degree of vulnerability of water resources and any conflicting demands along with their possible impacts on the aquatic environment.

Water statistics should be designed in the light of the policies promoting rational water use backed by explicit protection capability. The statistical system should thus map, describe and evaluate water resources and their use more as a means of facilitating their protection and sustainable management on a national level rather than as a basis for encouraging their exploitation. The system should be "problem-seeking" rather than "problem solving", as it should serve as an aid in the identification of areas of particular environmental significance, sectors and problems of water management of immediate or specific concern and zones of actual or potential conflict. This information should provide at an early stage considerable input to decision making and policy formulation but with a much wider range of information (e.g. on socio-economic, demographic and environmental aspects). It becomes evident that to serve these functions such a framework information system should go beyond merely providing an inventory of raw water data but should in addition offer a means for interpreting and evaluating the context of water statistics.

Comprehensive water data has to be collected on a periodic, nationwide basis or it would be impossible to assemble a complete cross-sectional and longitudinal data set for the various water users, or to assess water pollution and ambient water quality from existing data. While such time-series are well-established for hydrology and related fields they are almost non-existent for other sectors of water management. Without time-series, however, it would be difficult to identify trends in water-use behaviour or changes in ambient water quality and reduction in pollution discharged. It should also be borne in mind that measurements regarding water use and water quality not made now are lost forever; today's water use and ambient water quality cannot be measured in the future after further changes have taken place. It is therefore obvious that all countries, if they have not done so already, will have to establish at least a minimum programme to collect basic water management data on a routine basis.

NEED FOR INTEGRATION AND CO-ORDINATION

To satisfy the needs of users of water statistics requires not only development of specialized statistical systems on water use and water quality but also the transposition and adaptation of other related statistics by linking the data with socio-economic, demographic and environmental data-base. Despite the need for a higher degree of integration of water-related data, the fact remains that the demand is most articulated by specialized users. Nevertheless, a number of corresponding statistical sets is identified in the following list, randomly illustrating the range of statistics on the periphery of water management which now come to the fore and may require more attention in future; it should be noted that statistics on in-stream uses (navigation, hydroelectric production, fishery, recreation, etc.) and on hydrology including flood control are at the centre of water management.

(a) Land-use statistics: location of important water users and polluters; zoning; point and non-point sources of pollution; remote sensing techniques; environmental mapping; vulnerability maps, etc.

(b) Statistics for environmental impact assessment: evaluation of the effects on the aquatic environment of restructuring activities, engineering projects and other schemes as well as non-structural measures. The desirable characteristics of data for these purposes would be those that are suitable for ex-ante and/or ex-post analysis.

(c) Aquatic-ecosystem statistics: demand for this data arises from the growing recognition of the critical role of ecological equilibrium in long-term planning and its important contribution to the quality of life. Included in this group would be parameters that measure ecological stability, recoverability, resilience and information categories with particular significance to ambient water quality: the degree of eutrophication and saprobiation; bio-accumulation of toxic materials; changes in the biological composition of the ecosystem (species diversity retrogression, size distribution and population fluctuations).

(d) Environmental statistics for public information. The public has specific interests concerning the condition of the immediate environment. The need for access to highly localized data will therefore increase. There will furthermore be a demand for environmental indicators describing the environment, and specifically the aquatic environment, by means of summary statistics that are few in number, cover major environmental concerns and are easy to comprehend.

(e) Air-quality statistics: related to the acidification of lakes, soil and ground water, the impact of transportation processes, heavy metals and other toxic and resistant compounds in soils and their consequent pollution of ground water; potential transfer of pollutants from air-pollution control installations to the aquatic environment.

(f) Transportation statistics regarding dangerous goods: emergency cases with impact on water resources; remedial measures; comparison between different transportation methods, etc.

(g) Solid-waste statistics: origin, transport and treatment of solid wastes and potential accidents with consequent water pollution; discharge of solid wastes with consequent ground-water pollution; dumps, controlled landfill, containment, etc.

(h) Demographic statistics including tourist and migration statistics: to identify water-use patterns and sewage discharge practices; to evaluate water demand and pollution discharge in regions vulnerable to large-scale seasonal changes of population and to assess the need for water supply and sewerage infrastructure.

(i) Health statistics: to reveal any consequences and impacts of water pollution on human health and to analyse environmental causes of human morbidity and morality.

(j) Materials/Energy balance statistical systems: the statistical description of the fate of water pollutants from production stages to marketing, use, reuse, discharge and final concentration in the aquatic environment.

(k) Energy statistics: to show the correlation between energy and water statistics, both from a quantitative and qualitative point of view. Heat, for example, as a form of pollution, is of particular importance: thermal power plants are becoming a notable source of thermal pollution, especially along highly developed industrial river stretches.

The development of a statistical system on water use and water quality should involve statisticians and water managers as well as experts from the water users side together with exports from related fields. It is evident that an information system for water statistics as a whole should be based on precisely defined and realistic models of the complex and compound inter-disciplinary relationship between hydrology, ambient water quality, water uses both in-stream and off-stream as well as quality aspects of such uses. Such models should take into account the dynamic and changing nature of water management and related sectors and enable the information system to record these changes. Moreover, as environmental processes tend to operate independently of political or other man-made boundaries, this must be allowed for in the system.

Nevertheless all the complexity of the real world cannot be contained within a model: scientific models are themselves imperfect. In addition, other constraints, such as limitations of cost, time, data availability, manpower and technical experience mean that information systems themselves cannot be overly sophisticated but must simply comply with reality, without distorting it. For this reason an ideal system should not be too mechanistic.

NEED FOR COMPATIBILITY ON AN INTERNATIONAL LEVEL

Any exchange of experience among countries gained in integrated water management would require that statistical information be compatible, and that data be collected, processed and presented according to common rules using consistent terminology with agreed definitions. Only such preconditions will make national data on water resources and water use - including both quantity and quality aspects, as well as prevention of water pollution - directly comparable. This need was already emphasized by the Final Act of the Conference on Security and Co-operation in Europe (CSCE) by which participating States agreed, inter alia, "to increase the effectiveness of national and international measures for the protection of the environment, by the comparison and, if appropriate, the harmonization of methods of gathering and analysing facts, ... by the exchange of information, by the harmonization of definitions and the adoption, as far as possible, of a common terminology. ..."

For this national system of water statistics to work a common framework is needed. This could include elements of the same statistical information corresponding to the most important indicators of water management of international significance. Data collection, processing and presentation should be carried out according to compatible methods and agreed definitions. In the light of these considerations and with a view to assisting countries in elaborating such a framework statistical system on water use and water quality, the Committee on Water Problems, in co-operation with the Conference of European Statisticians and assisted by the Group of Experts on Aspects of Water Quality and Quantity have developed the system set out in the following chapter. In the view of the Committee the system should facilitate the best possible presentation of national statistical data so as to enhance their comparability on a national and international level.

II. UNIFORM SYSTEM OF WATER-USE STATISTICS

Since its inception, the Committee on Water Problems has paid particular attention to the development and application of water-use statistics with a view to identifying problems and examining possibilities for further action in regard to the rational use of water in the ECE region. In a first attempt, the Committee, at its fifth session (1973), endorsed a system of statistics applied in reviewing water use in ECE countries.

This system covers basic elements of water abstraction from surface water, ground water and other water resources for supply to population, industry, agriculture and for other purposes, in addition to water consumption in these user-categories. Provision has been made for further disaggregation of data into the following user components:

(a) Water from public water-supply systems;

(b) Individual water supply in rural areas (without piped water supply);

(c) Supply for industrial purposes from public water-supply systems;

(d) Supply for industry from its own water supply systems (including cooling water);

(e) Water delivered by industry to the population (to communities);

(f) Water for livestock (cattle watering, etc.);

(g) Water for irrigation;

(h) Water for fish-farming;

(i) Water for control of water levels;

(j) Water for other purposes (excluding waterways and hydropower production).

In order to ensure maximum comparability of water-use statistics it was recommended that the user categories be composed as follows: population (a+b-c+e); industry (d+c-e); agriculture (f+g+h) and other purposes (i+j). Deviations from this breakdown should be specified in individual national contributions.

In addition, the statistical system provides for more disaggregated information for (a) domestic, municipal, industrial and agricultural use of drinking water from public water supply; (b) total daily per capita use of water from public water supply systems and similar data for domestic use only per capita of entire population and/or per capita of population supplied from public water system; (c) water use and consumption in individual branches of industry (it was found desirable in this respect to use the International Standard Industrial Classification of All Economic Activities (ISIC)); (d) water use and consumption for industrial cooling, industrial processing, sanitary and service purposes in industry, etc.; and (e) once-through cooling in thermal power plants and in other branches of industry as well as circulation cooling in thermal power stations and other industries.

The Committee, at its fifteenth session in 1983, commenced elaborating a system of water-use statistics, in co-operation with the Conference of European Statisticians. The system, coherent with present and previous activities, was intended to facilitate the best possible presentation of all national statistical data regarding ex situ water use so as to enhance their comparability, both with regard to water quality and water quantity. The Work resulted in a unified system structured according to a sequence suggested by normal flow patterns of ex situ water utilization: abstraction, treatment prior to first use, supply, multiple use, recycling and re-use, consumption, discharge, collection, treatment and disposal of waste water, sludge treatment, disposal and reuse.

The uniform system appearing in the nine sheets which follow may be consulted in reference to the attached definitions of terms for use in systems of water statistics. In actual data reporting, appropriate multiples of the unit of measurements indicated in the following sheets should be used.

DEFINITIONS OF TERMS FOR USE IN SYSTEMS OF WATER STATISTICS

ABSTRACTION FEE

Payment for withdrawing water either per volume, per surface area or according to other criterion.

ADVANCED TREATMENT TECHNOLOGY

Process capable of reducing specific constituents in waste water or sludge not normally achieved by other treatment options. For the purpose of this classification, advanced treatment technology covers all unit operations which are not considered to be mechanical or biological. In waste-water treatment this includes e.g. chemical coagulation, flocculation and precipitation, break-point chlorination, stripping, mixed media filtration, micro-screening, selective ion exchange, activated carbon adsorption, reverse osmosis, ultra-filtration, electro flotation.

In sludge treatment this includes e.g. chemical conditioning, desinfection, filter pressing, vacuum filtration, centrifugation, incineration. Advanced treatment processes are also used in combination and/or in conjunction with mechanical and biological unit operations.

EXPENDITURE

Sum of gross fixed capital formation and expenditure for current operations related directly or indirectly to the protection, regulation, supply, treatment or discharge of water and treatment and disposal of sludge.

ARTIFICIAL GROUND-WATER RECHARGE

Diversion of water from surface and other sources into aquifers by means of settling basins, injection wells or other engineering works aimed at replenishing ground-water resources.

Sheet 1: Water abstraction from natural water resources

Means of abstraction	Raw water abstraction from					Total		Abstraction sites				Treatment prior to first use	
	Surface water	of which drinking water quality	Ground water	of which drinking water quality	Other sources (saline, brackish)	abstraction	of which drinking water quality	Surface water	Ground water	Other water resources	Total		
	m^3/y	m^3/y	m^3/y	m^3/y	m^3/y	m^3/y	m^3/y	number				m^3/y	% of [7]
1	2	3	4	5	6	7	8	9	10	11	12	13	14
a Water works													
b Domestic self-supply													
c Medicinal and mineral water exploitation													
d Subtotal [a + b + c]													
e Agricultural self-supply													
f Industrial self-supply													
g Water management (water level control, artificial ground-water recharge, etc.)													
h Heat recovery by heat pumps													
i Total [d + e + f + g + h]													

Recommended as essential statistical information

2 (a, b, e, f)
4 (a, b, e, f)
6 (a, b, e, f)

Sheet 2: Water supply, use and consumption in the domestic and municipal sector

Supply means and specific uses	Amount of water supplied of drinking water quality	Water consumption and losses	Return of water	Population concerned	Length of pipelines	Energy spent in supplying water	Expenditures for water supply	Revenue accruing to water management from abstraction fees and water charges	Subsidies for water supply
	m^3/y	m^3/y	m^3/y	number	km	MWh per year	national currency per year	national currency per year	national currency per year
1	2	3	4	5	6	7	8	9	10
a Supply from water works to population									
of which used for:									
b - Domestic purposes									
c - Municipal purposes									
d Domestic self-supply									
e Other supply									
f Total water supplied to population [a + d + e]									
g Total supply from water works									
of which supplied to:									
h - Agriculture									
i - Industry									

Recommended as essential information

a (2, 3, 4, 5)

g 2

Sheet 3: Water supply, use and consumption in the agricultural sector

Supply means and specific agricultural uses	Amount of water			Water consumption	Water losses during transportation	Return of water	Recycled water	Recycling coefficient	Surface irrigated km²
	of drinking water quality m³/y	of less than drinking water quality m³/y	total [2+3] m³/y	m³/y	m³/y	m³/y	m³/y		
1	2	3	4	5	6	7	8	9	10
a Agricultural self-supply									
b Supply from water works									
c Other supply (please specify)									
d Total water supplied [a+b+c] of which used in:									
e - large-scale intensive livestock farming									
f - Fish farming and similar activities									
g - Irrigation									

Recommended as essential statistical information

à (2, 3, 7)

Sheet 4: Water supply, use and consumption in the industrial sector

Supply means and specific industrial uses	Amount used as			Total [cols 2+3+ 4+5] m³/y	Water consumption and losses m³/y	Return of water m³/y	Recycled water m³/y	Recycling coefficient	Water saved by recycling m³/y
	Drinking water m³/y	Industrial process water and supplementary water m³/y	Cooling water m³/y	Other industrial use of water (please specify) m³/y						
1	2	3	4	5	6	7	8	9	10	11
a Industrial self-supply										
b Supply from water works										
c Other supply (please specify)										
d Subtotal (a+b+c)										
e Water delivered from industries to population										
f Total water available [d-e] of which used in the following categories:										
g Mining and quarrying ISIC 2										
h Food, beverage, etc. 31										
i Textile 321										
j Tanning and leather finishing 323										
k Pulp and paper, printing 34										
l Chemicals, petroleum, coal, rubber and plastic products 35										
m Iron, steel and non-ferrous metals basic industry 37										
n Fabricated metal products, machinery etc. incl. metal-plating 38										
o Thermal power plants 4101										
p Others (please specify)										

Recommended as essential statistical information

f (2, 3, 4, 7, 8, 9, 10)

Sheet 5: Discharge and collection of domestic sewage and storm water

Means of sewage collection	Amount discharged annually (m³/year and tons BOD per year)	Population concerned or population equivalent [p.e.] (number)	Discharge area total (km²)	Length of sewerage networks (km)	Waste water passing treatment plants — Portion of sewage effluent treated					Waste water not treated and discharged into	
					Total (m³/year)	Total (tons BOD per year)	Re-used by other water users (in % of [6])	Discharged into — Inland surface water or earth (in % of [6])	Discharged into — Sea (in % of [6])	Inland surface water or earth (m³/year and tons BOD per year)	Sea (m³/year and tons BOD per year)
1	2	3	4	5	6	7	8	9	10	11	12
a Discharge from domestic sector into public sewerage - of which into											
b - Combined sewerage											
c - Separate sewerage											
d Storm-water and surface water run-off from the domestic sector - of which collected in											
e - Combined sewerage											
f - Separate storm sewers											
g Discharge from dwellings not connected to public sewerage											
h Subtotal: Discharge of sewage and storm-water in combined sewerage											
i Total discharge of sewage and related storm-water in public sewerage											

Recommended as essential statistical information

2 (a, d, g)
i (3, 6, 7, 8, 9, 10, 11, 12)

Sheet 6: Treatment of waste water and storm water

	Origin	Amount actually treated	Pre-treatment	Total treatment plants	Capacity and size of treatment plants						Main treatment technology applied						Energy consumption for waste water collection and treatment	Treatment plant staff	National Expenditure for waste water collection and treatment per year	National Revenue accruing to water management from effluent charges per year	National Subsidies for waste water collection and treatment per year
					Small		Medium		Large		Mechanical		Biological		Advanced						
		m³/y	% of [2]	number	% of [2]	% of [4]	% of [2]	% of [4]	% of [2]	% of [4]	% of [2]	% of [4]	% of [2]	% of [4]	% of [2]	% of [4]	MWh/year	number	currency	currency	currency
	1	2	3	4	5	6	7	8	9	10	11	12	13	14	15	16	17	18	19	20	21
a	Public sewerage - of which from:																				
b	Industrial sewers discharging into public sewerage																				
c	Dwellings with individual outfalls, sewers																				
d	Storm-sewers																				

Recommended as essential statistical information

a (2, 4, 6, 8, 10, 11, 13, 15)

b 2

Sheet 7: Discharge and treatment of agricultural waste water

Origin of agricultural waste water	Amount discharged annually		Annual amount of treated waste water					Total water re-use	Agricultural enterprises with a treatment plant		Expenditures for waste water treatment	Revenue accruing to water management from effluent charges	Subsidies for waste water treatment
			Total		of which treated by the following technology								
		Population equivalent		Population equivalent	Mechanical	Biological	Advanced		number	under regular monitoring			
	m^3/y		m^3/y		% of [4]			m^3/y		% of [10]	national currency per year	national currency per year	national currency per year
1	2	3	4	5	6	7	8	9	10	11	12	13	14
a Total agricultural sector of which:													
b - large-scale, intensive livestock-farming													
c - Irrigation return flow													

Recommended as essential statistical information

a (2, 4, 6, 7, 8, 9)

Sheet 8: Discharge and treatment of industrial process waste water and cooling water

Origin of industrial process waste water and cooling water		Annual amount discharged		Annual amount treated together with domestic sewage		Annual amount treated by industries					Total water re-used	Industrial enterprises with treatment plants		Expenditures for waste water treatment	Revenue accruing to water management from effluent charges	Subsidies for waste water treatment
						Total		of which treated by the following technology in % of [6]								
	ISIC		Population equivalent		Population equivalent		Population equivalent	Mechanical	Biological	Advanced		number	under regular monitoring % of [12]			
		m^3/y		m^3/y		m^3/y					m^3/y			national currency per year	national currency per year	national currency per year
1		2	3	4	5	6	7	8	9	10	11	12	13	14	15	16
a Total industrial process waste water																
b - of which from Mining and quarrying	2															
c - Food, beverage, etc	31															
d - Textile	321															
e - Tanning and leather finishing	323															
f - Pulp and paper printing	34															
g - Chemicals, petroleum, coal, rubber and plastic products	35															
h - Iron, steel and non-ferrous metal basic industry	37															
i - Fabricated metal production etc.	38															
j - Others (please specify)																
k Total cooling water of which from	2+3															
l - Industrial processes																
m - Thermal power plants	4101															

Recommended as essential statistical information

a (2, 6, 8, 9, 10, 11)

k (2, 6, 11)

Sheet 9: Sludge treatment, disposal and re-use.

Sludge origin		Annual amount of sludge generated	Total	Annual amount treated of which by the following technology:			Destination of sludge									Expenditures for sludge treatment and disposal	Subsidies for sludge treatment and disposal
				Mechanical	Biological	Advanced	Dumping, sanitary landfill		Re-use in agriculture				Re-use in industry (please specify)		Other (please specify):			
									as compost		spray irrigation							
		tons dry matter content	tons dry matter content		% of [3]	% of [3]	% of [2]	% of [3]	% of [2]	% of [3]	% of [2]	% of [3]	% of [2]	% of [3]	% of [2]	% of [3]	national currency per year	national currency per year
1		2	3	4	5	6	7	8	9	10	11	12	13	14	15	16	17	18
a	Water works																	
b	Sewage and storm water treatment																	
c	Subtotal																	
d	Industrial process waste water treatment of which: ISIC																	
e	- Mining and quarrying 2																	
f	- Food, beverage, etc. 31																	
g	- Textile 321																	
h	- Tanning and leather finishing 323																	
i	- Pulp and paper, printing 34																	
j	- Chemicals, petroleum, coal, rubber and plastic products 35																	
k	- Iron, steel and non-ferrous metals basic industry 37																	
l	- Fabricated metal products machinery, etc. incl. metal-plating 38																	
m	- others (please specify)																	
o	- Cooling water treatment in industries and thermal power plants																	

Recommended as essential statistical information

c (2, 3, 4, 5, 6)
d (2, 3, 4, 5, 6)

AVERAGE LONG-TERM ANNUAL INFLOW INTO COUNTRY

Inflow of surface waters into a country, annual data averaged over a period of at least 20 consecutive years.

AVERAGE LONG-TERM ANNUAL RESIDUAL ATMOSPHERIC PRECIPITATION

Average annual residual atmospheric precipitation over a long period, normally 20 years or more. The item refers to the total annual atmospheric precipitation over the area after adjustment for evaporation and transpiration.

AVERAGE LONG-TERM ANNUAL RUN-OFF ORIGINATING IN COUNTRY

Outflow of surface waters from a country, annual data averaged over a period of at least 20 consecutive years.

BANK FILTRATION

Induced infiltration of river water through bankside gravel strata (by pumping from wells sunk into the gravel strata to create a hydraulic gradient) with the intention of improving the water quality. For purpose of the classification, bank filtration is covered under surface water.

BIOCHEMICAL OXYGEN DEMAND (BOD)

The mass concentration of dissolved oxygen consumed under specific conditions by the biological oxidation of organic and/or inorganic matter in water.

BIOLOGICAL TREATMENT TECHNOLOGY

Processes which employ aerobic or anaerobic micro-organisms and result in decanted effluents and separated sludge containing microbial mass together with pollutants. Biological treatment processes are also used in combination and/or in conjunction with mechanical and advanced unit operations.

CAPACITY OF RESERVOIRS USED FOR FLOOD CONTROL

Maximum total retention volume of water reservoirs, either natural or artificial, which are used, exclusively or in combination with other uses, for flood control. Average available capacity of such reservoirs for flood-control purposes refers to the part of total capacity which is available to flood control over an annual average of 20 or more consecutive years.

CAPACITY AND SIZE OF TREATMENT PLANTS

For this statistical system, the following size ranges of treatment plants are recognized:

Small - 500 to 10,000 population equivalent (p.e.) or 150 to 3,000 m^3 per day dry weather flow (DWF)

Medium - 10,000 to 100,000 p.e. or 3,000 to 30,000 m^3 per day DWF

Large - greater than 100,000 p.e. or greater than 30,000 m^3 per day DWF.

CHLOROPHYLL A CONTENT

Content of chlorophyll a in a given unit of water. It is an indication of the existing biomass of the phytoplankton and the periphyton in a water body (mg/m^3 or mg/m^2).

COMBINED SEWERAGE

A system in which waste water and surface water are carried in the same drains and sewers.

CONCENTRATION

Concentration is expressed as the specific content of a parameter per specified unit of water or waste water.

COOLING WATER

Water which is used to adsorb and remove heat. In this classification cooling water is broken down into cooling water used in the generation of electricity in thermal power stations, and cooling water used in other industrial processes.

COOLING WATER TREATMENT

Process to render cooling water fit to meet applicable environmental standards or other quality norms for recycling or reuse.

DEPENDABLE SURFACE WATER RESOURCES AT 95 PER CENT OF TIME

Portion of the surface-water resource that can be depended on for annual water development during 19 out of 20 consecutive years, or at least 95 per cent of the years included in longer consecutive periods. This item yields information about the average annual long-term availability of surface waters for use in human activities.

DISCHARAGE AREA

Territory serviced by public sewerage.

DOMESTIC SEWAGE

Water discharged after use in households, municipalities, and community, social and personal services (ISIC 9). For purposes of this classification, industrial, commercial and trade waste water, which cannot be reported separately, is included in domestic sewage.

DRINKING WATER

Water of a quality suitable for drinking purposes.

FLOOD ENCROACHMENT AREA

Total land surface exposed to a substantial risk of being flooded by surface waters, including the sea. The flood encroachment area may or may not be protected or regulated by flood control measures. Tide tables are not included in this item.

GENERATION OF ELECTRICITY FROM HYDROPOWER

Electrical energy production from hydropower stations, whether or not involving temporary withdrawals of water from its course, including the production from pumped storage operations, assessed at the heat value of electricity (3.6 TJ/GWh).

GOODS CARRIED

Goods which have been moved by an Inland Water Transport (IWT) craft on the network of inland waterways of the country concerned. The total quantity of goods carried in a country comprises the quantity of goods loaded in the country, the quantity of goods having entered the country by IWT and the quantity of goods in transit by IWT throughout.

GROSS FIXED CAPITAL FORMATION

The outlays (purchases and own-account production) of industries, producers of government services and producers of private non-profit services to households, additions of new durable goods (commodities) to their stocks of fixed assets less their net sales of similar second-hand and scrapped goods. Included are acquisitions of reproducible and non-reproducible durable goods (except land, mineral deposits, timber tracts and the like) for civilian use; work-in-progress on construction projects; capital repairs; outlays on the improvement of land; and the transfer costs in connection with purchases and sales of land, etc.

GROUND WATER

Water which is being held in, and can usually be recovered from, or via, an underground formation. All permanent and temporary deposits of water, both artificially charged and naturally, in the subsoil, being of sufficient quality for at least seasonal use. This category includes phreatic water-bearing strata, as well as deep strata under pressure or not, contained in porous or fracture soils. For purposes of this classification, ground water includes springs, both concentrated and diffused, which may be subaqueous. Excluded from ground water is bank filtration (covered under surface water).

GROUND-WATER RESOURCES

The availability of ground water for water development depends on technical, economic and environmental considerations. Technically available ground water is that portion of total ground water that can be adapted using available technology. Economically available ground water refers to that part of technically available ground water that may be withdrawn from the resource

at prevailing production costs. Environmentally available ground water
relates to the part of total ground water that may be abstracted without major
undesirable effects upon natural habitats.

HEAT RECOVERY

Abstraction of thermal energy from water by exploiting the heat potential
of water using heat pumps followed by direct return of water to the original
water resource.

INDUSTRIAL PROCESS WATER

Any water used for, or during an industrial process.

INDUSTRIAL PROCESS WASTE-WATER

Water discharged after being used in, or produced by, industrial
production processes which is of no further immediate value to these
processes. Where process water recycling systems have been installed, process
waste-water is the final discharge from these circuits. To meet quality
standards for eventual discharge into public sewers, this process waste-water
is understood to be subjected to ex-process in-plant treatment (see
PRETREATMENT). Cooling water is not considered to be process waste-water for
purposes of this classification. Sanitary waste-water and surface run-off
from industries are also excluded here.

INLAND WATER TRANSPORT CRAFT

Craft having a minimum carrying capacity of 20 tonnes, designed for the
carriage of goods by inland waterway.

IN-STREAM WATER USE

Use made of a body of water without abstracting water from it. In-stream
uses include navigation, hydroelectric power generation, the provision of
habitats for fish and other wildlife, aesthetic enjoyment, other recreational
uses.

IRRIGATION RETURN FLOW

Irrigation water not consumed but returned to inland water resources.

IRRIGATION WATER

Water which is applied to soils in order to increase their moisture
content and to provide for normal plant growth. For purposes of the
classification, data reported under this item fit in ISIC major division 1.

MECHANICAL TREATMENT TECHNOLOGY

Processes of a physical and mechanical nature which result in decanted
effluents and separate sludge. Mechanical processes are also used in
combination and/or in conjunction with biological and advanced unit
operations. Mechanical treatment is understood to include at least such
processes as sedimentation, flotation, etc.

MEDICINAL AND MINERAL WATER EXPLOITATION

Abstraction, treatment, distribution, sale and use of water suitable for medicinal purposes or mineral water consumption.

MONITORING

The programmed process of sampling, measurement and subsequent recording or signalling, or both, of various water characteristics, often with the aim of assessing conformity to specified objectives.

NAVIGABLE INLAND WATERWAYS

A stretch of water, not part of the sea, over which craft of a carrying capacity not less than 50 tonnes can navigate when normally loaded. This term covers both navigable rivers and lakes (natural watercourses, whether or not they have been improved for navigation purposes) and navigable canals (waterways constructed primarily for the purpose of navigation). The length of lakes is counted as that between the most distant points between which transport is performed.

NOT PROTECTED/REGULATED

Flood encroachment area not subject to any protective or preventive measure within the scope of flood-control efforts.

NUMBER OF LICENSED RECREATIONAL FISHERMEN

Number of licensed fishermen who are not counted among the labour force employed in commercial fishing.

OTHER INDUSTRIAL PROCESS WATER

All industrial process water except cooling water.

OTHER INDUSTRIAL USE OF WATER

Use of water in industrial establishments for purposes not otherwise specified.

OTHER PREVENTIVE/PROTECTIVE MEASURES

Flood encroachment area subject to flood-control measures not covered by protection through landscape restructuring nor preventive regulation. Included in this category are also those parts of the flood encroachment area which are controlled through a combination of flood-control measures as defined in this classification.

OTHER SUPPLY

Any supply of water not specified elsewhere. In particular, supplies from commercial and industrial establishments, whether marketed or not, are covered under this item. Also included is supply of reused water.

OTHER WATER

Includes atmospheric precipitation, sea water, permanent bodies of stagnant water both natural and artificial, mine water, drainage water (reclamations) and transitional water, such as brackish swamps, lagoons and estuarine areas. Resources can be assessed statistically for individual components of other water, but not for the item as a whole. Thus, data to be included in the balance of water resources and needs are confined to abstractions and consumption. Other water resources may be of great importance locally, although in a national context they are usually of less importance compared to surface- and ground-water resources.

POPULATION EQUIVALENT (p.e.)

The number of persons producing, under "normal domestic" or "standard" conditions, sewage of certain chracteristics.

PRETREATMENT

Process to render waste water and storm water fit to meet quality standards prior to its discharge into sewers.

PROTECTION THROUGH LANDSCAPE RESTRUCTURING

Flood encroachment area for which the risk of being flooded is reduced through the physical regulation of rivers, the construction of reservoirs used for purposes of flood control, whether located inside or outside the flood-encroachment area, dikes and dams and any other construction of installations serving the same purpose. Excluded are those parts of the thus protected flood-encroachment area which are at the same time subject to other flood-control measures as defined in this classification.

PUBLIC SEWERAGE

Sewerage networks operated by governmental, federal or local authorities, by communities, water authorities or sewage/waste-water collection, discharge and treatment associations.

PUBLIC WATER SUPPLY

Water supply by water works. Deliveries of water from one public supply undertaking to another are excluded.

QUALITY CHARACTERISTICS OF WASTE-WATER

Quality characteristics are expressed either in terms of quantity of specific substances or in terms of concentrations of such substances. In reporting on heavy metals, toxic organic compounds, as well as on other biological indicators, the specific substances or parameters concerned should be clearly stated.

QUANTITY

The quantity of a given substance (expressed in tonnes) discharged during one year into the aquatic environment, including the sea (total load).

RAIN WATER

Water arising from atmospheric precipitation, which has not yet collected soluble matter from the soil.

RAW WATER

Water which has received no treatment whatsoever, or water entering a plant for further treatment.

RECYCLED WATER

Water that is used more than once by the same user inside semi-closed or closed circuits for the same purpose or for different purposes.

RECYCLING COEFFICIENT

Ratio of water volume needed theoretically by the same water user for production or cooling processes in the absence of recycling systems in relation to the volume of water actually supplied for a given purpose and for a given time period. Water heating systems (either industrial or domestic) are excluded.

RETURN OF WATER

Water discharged into inland water resources after use. Discharges include cooling water, waste-water, storm water, irrigation return flow, etc. In general, the volume of returned water establishes the balance between water abstractions, water consumption and water losses.

REUSED WATER see WATER REUSE

REVENUE ACCRUING TO WATER MANAGEMENT

Total amount of monies collected and received by water authorities.

SELF-SUPPLY

Abstraction of water, its distribution and use outside public water supply systems.

SEPARATE SEWERAGE

Sewers which collect either domestic sewage or storm water in separate conduits.

SEWAGE EFFLUENT

Treated sewage discharged from a sewage treatment plant.

SLUDGE

The accumulated settled solids separated from various types of water either moist or mixed with a liquid component as a result of natural or artificial processes.

SLUDGE TREATMENT

Process to render sludge fit to meet applicable environmental standards, land-use regulations or other quality norms for recycling or reuse. Three broad types of treatment are distinguished in the classification: mechanical, biological and advanced treatment. Such treatment not only reduces volume but also stabilizes and transforms the residue into environmentally acceptable components and useful by-products.

STORM WATER = STORM WATER RUN-OFF

Surface water draining to sewers or to a watercourse as a result of heavy rainfall.

STORM WATER COLLECTED

Portion of storm water run-off which enters either combined sewerage or separate storm sewers for further treatment, reuse or discharge.

STORM WATER TREATMENT

Process to render storm water fit to meet applicable environmental standards or other quality norms for recylcing or reuse.

SUBSIDY

Assistance in cash or in kind, usually provided by a State to local, regional or other authorities, firms or private persons.

SUPPLY OF WATER

Delivery of water to final users or own-abstraction of water for final use (self-supply).

SURFACE WATER

Water which flows over, or rests on the surface of a land mass: natural watercourses such as rivers, streams, brooks, lakes, etc., as well as artificial watercourses such as irrigation, industrial and navigation canals, drainage systems and artificial reservoirs. For purposes of this classification, bank filtration is covered under surface water but sea-water, permanent bodies of stagnant water both natural and artificial, and transitional waters, such as brackish swamps, lagoons and estuarine areas are not considered surface water and so are included under OTHER WATER.

TREATED WASTE WATER

Waste water discharged from treatment plant (= effluent).

TREATMENT PLANT

Installation to render waste water, sludge, storm water or cooling water fit to meet applicable environmental standards or other quality norms for recycling or reuse.

TREATMENT PLANT STAFF

Persons employed in treatment plants.

TREATMENT PRIOR TO FIRST USE

Process to render water drawn from any source suitable for first use. For purposes of the classification, simple screening of water is not considered treatment.

WASTE WATER

Water which is of no further immediate value to the purpose for which it was used or in the pursuit of which it was produced because of its quality, quantity or time of occurrence. However, waste water from one user can be a potential supply to a user elsewhere. Cooling water is not considered to be waste water for purposes of this classification.

WASTE WATER NOT TREATED

Waste water discharged into ambient media without treatment.

WASTE WATER TREATMENT

Process to render waste water fit to meet applicable environmental standards or other quality norms for recycling or reuse. Three broad types of treatment are distinguished in the classification: mechanical, biological and advanced. For purposes of calculating the total amount of treated waste water, volumes reported should be shown only under the "highest" type of treatment to which it was subjected. Thus, waste water treated mechanically as well as biologically should be shown under biological treatment, and waste water treated in accordance with all three types should be reported under advanced treatment.

WATER ABSTRACTION

Removal of water from any source, either permanently or temporarily is known as abstraction. Mine water and drainage water are excluded.

WATER CHARGES

Payment for use of water.

WATER CONSUMPTION

Water abstracted which is no longer available for use because it has evaporated, transpired, been incorporated into products and crops, consumed by man or livestock, ejected directly to the sea, or otherwise removed from freshwater resources. Water losses during the transport of water between the point or points of abstraction and the point or points of use are excluded.

WATER LEVEL CONTROL

Water diverted from surface water, ground water and other water to replenish a particular water body with a view to securing minimum or maximum flow and the necessary water level for various in-stream uses.

WATER LOSS DURING TRANSPORT

Volume of water lost during transport between a point of abstraction and a point of use, or between points of use and reuse.

WATER POLLUTION CONTROL

Includes industrial effluent treatment, sewage treatment (but not collection), marine oil spill controls and drinking water treatment that goes beyond that for public health purposes (e.g. carbon filtration, denitrification).

WATER RECYCLING

Repeated use of the same water by the same user. The product of the volume of the water recycled and the recycling coefficient defines the amount of water saved through the application of water recycling systems and is equivalent to the total use made of water supplied.

WATER RESOURCE

Amount of water available for water development in a country during a specified time period.

WATER REUSE

Repeated use of the same water by subsequent users in sequential systems between initial abstraction and discharge. Between successive uses, the water may or may not undergo treatment. If total water reused is measured, volumes are counted in full for each successive user.

WATER SAVED BY RECYCLING

Difference between the volume of actually used water and the volume of water that would have been theoretically needed had recycling not been applied.

WATER SUPPLY see SUPPLY OF WATER

WATER USE

Utilization of water for specific purposes.

WATER USED FOR DOMESTIC PURPOSES

Water used for normal household purposes.

WATER USED FOR MUNICIPAL PURPOSES

Water used for the normal purposes of community, social and personal services (ISIC 9), including water used for the purposes of public adminsitrations (e.g. street cleaning, watering of green areas, fire fighting).

WATER USER

User categories are defined in terms of the International Standard Industrial Classification of all Economic Activities (ISIC), except for user category "domestic sector", which includes households, municipalities, and community, social and personal services (ISIC 9).

WATER WORKS

Facility to abstract raw water from a source, treat it according to standard procedures (treatment prior to first use) and supply it to water users on a commercial basis.

WATER WORKS AND SUPPLY

Activities classified in ISIC division 42 and in COFOG group 07.2.

WEIGHT OF TOTAL LANDINGS IN COMMERCIAL FISHING

Total catch of fish and water plants from inland waters by professional fishermen.

PART B: SURVEYS OF NATIONAL SYSTEMS OF WATER STATISTICS

I.   STATISTICS TO VERIFY RATIONAL USE OF WATER

This section reviews country-by-country the present situation and outlook regarding national systems of water-use statistics for both quantity and quality. To a great extent the information has been provided by ECE Governments following a set of guidelines for the preparation of country monographs which the Committee on Water Problems had agreed upon at its thirteenth session.

The different components of water-use statistics applied in various countries are described. The experience gained in some countries in dealing with the problems and constraints encountered in applying such statistics is also reflected. In discussing the different statistical systems, attention has been given in particular to water-use statistics covering both quantity and quality data on abstraction, make-up, use, reuse, treatment and discharge of waste water. Reference has also been made to governmental policies aimed at streamlining, strengthening and rendering more efficient the future systems of water-use statistics on a country-wide level.

No account was taken in the survey of flood statistics nor of statistical systems or national surveys covering in situ water uses, such as navigation, timber floating or hydropower production because these deal with hydrographic information only in terms of quantity. Ambient water quality statistics derive from quality monitoring of both surface waters and ground-water aquifers are considered in chapter II of Part B.

In most ECE countries the central statistical office assumes the main responsibility at the national level for collecting and processing socio-economic data on population, production and income. Although important, this information is not sufficient for water-resource planning and management. Apart from conducting its own fundamental and applied research on water-related subjects, the statistical office usually delegates to expert agencies the tasks of drawing up and keeping special statistics. They publish these records either in their own name or jointly with the central statistical office.

The example of Finland may serve to illustrate this approach. In Finland the National Board of Waters is the agency responsible for statistics dealing with the quantity and quality of water resources and municipal and industrial water supply and effluent discharges. However, statistics on radio-active discharges are published by the Institute on Radiation Protection, statistics on water traffic, including timber floating and waterways, are kept by the Roads and Waterways Administration. Data concerning production of water power are collected and published by the Ministry of Trade and Industry, whereas fisheries statistics are the responsibility of the Finnish Game and Fisheries Research Institute. Statistics on summer cottages are kept by the central statistical office, like environmental statistics, which also contain data on water resources and their use.

In general, public water supply and sewage treatment companies and associations, as well as industries, thermal power stations, agricultural enterprises, and other water users keep detailed information on the use of water, including its supply and future demand, make-up, reuse, and final

treatment. Water authorities therefore have attempted in some countries to
collect and use these data. Some have established relevant surveys which
cover either (a) enterprises for public water supply and sewage treatment or
(b) water users (usually broken down by private households, industries,
agricultural and in situ uses, such as fishing and recreation) or possibly
both. In the latter case, the surveys would be supply- and user-oriented.
Data collection is carried out in most countries through questionnaires and
specially designed forms and with the help of local and district water
authorities. This methodology assures relatively harmonious reporting of
information and comparability of data on a provincial or national level.

It would be presumptuous to suggest that any one data programme is better
than another since each has its special purpose in the overall scheme of water
management. However, highest priority in data collection is usually accorded
to areas where problems are apparent or anticipated or where rapid changes are
occurring or expected. Only those countries with a well consolidated system
of statistics of a sufficiently long time series can respond rapidly to the
needs of keeping under control all aspects of water use. An immediate need
for data collection in specific fields of water management would pose great
problems in those countries where there is no infrastructure for data
collection on a national level or where relevant legal provisions are not
sufficient to allow for the implementation of an urgent data collection
programme. This would impede a sound statistical background for the
formulation of water policies or for the development of standards and
guidelines for decision-making. The importance of water statistics as a main
tool in integrated water management is underscored in chapter I of Part A
above.

In all countries, efforts therefore must continue towards efficient
co-ordination of collection and processing of data on water use and quality.
Moreover these water statistics have to be linked with the general information
system of the country. Unification of the reporting system on water use and
quality will vigorously diminish a certain user disparity and help overcome
the different and variable access to information which various administrations
have to date. Only systematic evaluation of water-use and quality data within
a uniform system will enable a rapid identification of changes as they arise
or explain their causes and indicate the relevant measures to be adopted.
This is increasingly significant when attempting to apply the principles of
rational water use and water pollution control, on a national and
international level. A uniform system of water-use statistics is presented in
chapter II of Part A above.

Owing to the variety of different statistical systems established in a
number of ECE countries for recording changes in water use and treatment
practices in the main economic sectors, the examples which follow are given
country-by-country. This is done not only to illustrate the various systems
but also to present experience gained during their application.

AUSTRIA

The Austrian Federal Institute for Water Quality is exploring all aspects
of water quality. To this end, the Institute is compiling a card index
containing data on surface waters, waste water discharge and purification
facilities. These data, however, are supplied sporadically. They are taken
into account when elaborating water quality descriptions such as

classification maps or surveys. In addition, institutes for sanitary investigation are watching over, inter alia, drinking water and bathing water quality. The Austrian Federal Institute for Plant Protection along with research institutes for agricultural chemistry are dealing with water-borne chemical residuals. The Federal Register on Water Management was entrusted with the elaboration of a national survey regarding the situation of water management. To this effect, all available data, studies and plans would have to be taken into account. If data are missing, the Register may supplement basic material needed with the assistance of technical universities and experts. Water statistics, in the most general sense of the term, exist as follows:

(a) Administration:

  - Quantitative data provided by the Hydrographical Service;

  - Studies prepared by the Water Management Register;

  - Regional statistics within the scope of federal provinces;

  - Reports of the Water Quality Surveillance Services;

  - Joint bilateral compilation concerning transboundary waters drawn up by the Federal Institute for Water Quality.

(b) Economic sector:

  - Sectoral statistics prepared by interested agencies and offices;

  - Special statistical data collected by individual associations and companies.

(c) Public statistics (inter alia, for use by mass media) drawn up by the Central Board on Statistics and by the specialized statistical institutes.

Apart from hydrographical statistics only partial statistics exist on water use and quality for specific economic sectors. This includes overall surveys which constitute statistics only in a very general sense. It applies in particular to studies carried out by the Water Management Register and to certain results reported by the Federal Institute for Water Quality and studies prepared at the local and provincial level. This information, provided regionally or in specialized fields, is only partly comparable and not always suitable for further evaluation. In addition, their availability can be limited. Indeed, as far as computerized data collection and processing is concerned, the Austrian Law on Data Protection specifies the degree of restriction which has to be guaranteed for person-related data and for the protection of industrial technology.

Experiences regarding problems and constraints encountered with the collection of water-use statistics are mainly being gained by users in municipal and industrial water management as well as in agriculture. For water works, difficulties arise in estimating the development of water demand and the shares of different end-users. In addition, overlapping in various data systems has been generating difficulties in distinguishing between public supply and private water-abstraction sources, particularly, as far as industrial branches are concerned. The compilation of data on waste-water discharges requires more effort than the collection of water-quality data. Industrial data on the regional as well as on the overall national level cannot usually be collected directly together with water-management statistics, but have rather to be derived from economic statistics as far as possible. For the purpose of water management, such material is only of limited significance and accuracy.

The existing legal provisions as contained in the Federal Act on Water Law together with administrative ordinances on establishing the Water Management Register of Austria do not form a sufficient basis for the collection and processing of data urgently required for water management. This is the main reason why obligations concerning the systematic collection and processing of water-related data have been stipulated for inclusion in the Federal Water Act. The scope of water-management planning should also be extended. To this end, water statistics and water-management planning should constitute a continuous process whereby information can be easily obtained or additional information can be fed back for elaboration. This final goal can only be achieved through suitable legislation and an appropriate administrative infrastructure.

BULGARIA

In the context of State statistics, regular statistical accounts have existed since 1952 of water supplies for community and household purposes. These accounts are intended to facilitate study of the volume of water distributed by the public supply system and the quantities used to meet drinking water, household and industrial needs. The reference units for the survey are the departmental undertakings for the supply of water to the localities.

To meet the needs for statistical data combined with the maintenance of a constant balance between the unified plan for water economy and economic sector development, the Committee on the Unified Social Information System of the People's Republic of Bulgaria has organized and introduced, as from 1978, a new form of statistical accounts for the annual study on water consumption in the economy as a whole.

The survey was organized in order to ensure that information was available for the social administration bodies as needed for administrative decisions and the formulation of policy for a complex and rational use of water resources and the protection of the ownership of surface and underground water.

Water use is studied with regard to factories, farms and organizations. The survey concerns industry, building, farming, forestry and transport undertakings, productive and non-productive organizations and those establishments in the economy as a whole whose annual volume of water used exceeds 100,000 cubic metres. The statistical accounts include electric power stations (hydroelectric, thermal and nuclear power stations) regardless of the fact that the water they use returns to the reservoirs and that the quantities actually consumed are only those taken to offset losses. At the present time, the sphere of factories, farms and organizations is considered sufficiently representative to provide the information required to study the problems of water consumption in the economy as a whole.

The statistical survey of water use covers: (a) quantities of water received from users, according to water resources; (b) quantities of water used by the main centres of users; (c) type and quality of water used for production purposes; and (d) volume and type of used water resulting from production and household activities of users.

The assessments of water consumption take the form of a balance sheet in which water resources and expenditure are recorded. This permits a relatively high degree of reliability in the data.

The supply of water is classified in statistics as follows:

Own water supply (water facilities built, exploited and maintained by the user);

Public water supply systems (drinking water supplied to users without regard for its subsequent use);

Other economic systems for water (facilities not owned by water users such as irrigation systems and water supply systems for technical purposes);

Supply of used water to other undertakings (water which, after use, is passed to the user-undertaking in question to meet production or irrigation needs or for purification).

The volume of water used is presented according to the purpose: production; irrigation; and drinking water and household supply of the personnel of the user-undertakings. Owing to considerations of a practical nature, the volumes of water used in the latter case include water used for these purposes in production undertakings, as well as the total water consumption of the undertakings, organizations and establishments in the non-productive sphere (undertakings which provide personal and community services to the population, nurseries, schools, cultural, health and sports establishments, convalescent homes, hotels, etc.). The concepts of "drinking water" and "process water" are defined according to the criterion of whether quality of the water used corresponds to the standards for drinking water in force in the country. Water which does not meet drinking water standards is considered to be "process" water and is classified as fresh water, consecutively reused water or recycled water. The quantities of consecutively reused and recycled water are recorded together. Thus the survey can record what volumes of water would be indispensable should the redistribution and supply systems fail, that is, it can evaluate the fresh water savings as a result of the installation of these systems.

Quantities of used water resulting from production and domestic activities are presented according to the following: conditionally pure water; water purified according to standard practices: of which by: mechanical; physical/chemical; and biological means; as well as polluted water.

Conditionally pure water is water which is not polluted in the course of its use in the technological production process and when discharged does not cause further pollution of the recipient.

The concept of "water purified according to standard practices" includes used water whose discharge following purification does not surpass prescribed quality standards. For practical reasons, the method used is to register purified used water only once, after the final stage of purification. The quality of used water takes account only of water which, in the course of its use, is polluted by various components and discharged into the recipient without purification, and water of which the degree of purification does not correspond to the relevant standards.

The factories, farms and organizations covered by the water consumption accounts draw up reports according to the questionnaire adopted and the instructions for completing it. These reports are submitted for verification to the territorial information and calculation centres of the Committee for the Unified Social Information System and then sent to the above Committee for centralized data processing. At the present stage, the tabulation programme of the results of the statistical survey on water consumption contains groupings for the country as a whole, by main economic sectors (industry, agriculture and all other sectors) and by ministries.

With regard to the breakdown by sectors, the distribution of water-users is effected on the basis of the sector to which the main activity of the undertaking or organization can be referred. The centralized processing of the data makes it possible to draw up extra tabulations so as to satisfy the information needs in this area of the largest possible number of users. For example, a group of reports on water consumption is established, excluding water used by electric power stations, reused water and recycled water, so as to obtain the volume of water actually consumed. During the preparation of the statistical balance on water, the data from the survey on water consumption for the whole of the economy is complemented by the data collected by the accounts for drinking water used by the population and taken from the public supply system.

The establishment of reports on water consumption is accompanied by certain difficulties mainly connected with the duplicated calculation of the volumes of water used by two subsequent users or of the volumes of recycled water, and particularly with the direct measurement of own-source water consumed, i.e. water not paid for.

In order to avoid duplicating calculations of the volumes of water used, it has been decided that the hydroelectric power generating stations should mention in their statistical reports only the volumes of water used for energy production (excluding irrigation and distribution), i.e. omitting the volumes of water which pass through the turbines of the power station and then on to agricultural organizations for irrigation or to other consumers.

The hydroelectric power stations are considered final users of these volumes of water and so record the quantities. Power stations in series record only the volume of water treated by the last power station, i.e. that located at the last step downstream, and not the volume of water which passes through the turbines of all the power stations. Using the same considerations, it has been decided that, when the recycled water is recorded, the volume of water which reaches the factory-floor and not that of the outflow is to be taken into account. Thermal and nuclear power stations, for example, include in the volume of recycled water only the quantities which enter their installations from reservoirs and cooling towers. The water sent

to the cooling towers, the steam distributed to factories and the hot water
which goes to water supply system users is not included, since it is
considered as outgoing recycled water. Of course, the methodology requires
some further refinement in this respect.

The problem of measuring the volumes of water used has not been entirely
resolved. There are farming and industrial users which do not have any
apparatus for directly measuring the water they use and receive from their own
sources. In the absence of such apparatus, at the present stage the water
used is measured by indirect means. For example, when water consumption is
accompanied by the pumping of underground water, the volumes used are
determined by the flow-rate of the pumps. A recording system is set up for
the operation of the pumping stations. When reporting on the volumes of water
used for energy production, the electric power stations apply what is known as
the specific water volume method, i.e. they make an evaluation on the basis of
the volume required to produce one kilowatt of electrical energy. Where it is
not possible to make direct measurements, hydrolytic calculations are made to
measure the volumes of water used.

It is obvious that the difficulties mentioned in connection with the
calculation of water consumption in Bulgaria are being gradually overcome, and
the statistical reports are thus being stabilized and improved so as to attain
the objectives and perform the tasks in view.

CANADA

A data base for the municipal sector, designated MUNDAT, has been
developed. It is designed to maintain an accurate account of municipal water
supply, treatment and waste-water treatment. The system is capable of
retrieving data in various formats and/or providing aggregate statistics on
selected data elements. The data base is accessible through time-sharing
terminals across the country. In addition to the municipal data base, the
Industrial Water Effluent Database has been established. It is in a
computerized data bank referred to as WATENIS, the Water Effluent National
Information System. The system consists of a collection of water-effluent
data bases. The data include effluent sources, the quality and quantity of
effluents discharged, as well as problems associated with their discharge.
These data form the background for the development of controls of pollutants
at source under National Baseline Effluent Controls. The controls are applied
uniformly nationally. The following specific water quality surveys are also
being carried out:

(a) Phosphorus control: A national sample collection and analysis
programme has been organized to ensure that detergent manufacturers and
importers comply with the regulations. In addition, other cleaning agents
which are not regulated at present are analysed for informational purposes.

(b) Environmental emergencies: To aid in the analysis of trends in
environmental emergencies, a computerized system known as the National
Analysis of Trends in Emergencies (NATES) has been developed. It includes
spill locations, type and quantity of material spilled, water bodies affected
and cause of the incident. The data are used primarily in promoting accident
prevention but can also aid in environmental impact studies and water-quality
assessments.

(c) <u>Pollution from land-use activities</u>: As part of the Great Lakes Water Quality Agreement between Canada and the United States (1972), an inventory of existing land uses for the Great Lakes Basin has been prepared with an emphasis on certain projects in the period 1980 and 2020. Specialized land uses having a high pollution potential have been identified and data on soil, geology, geomorphology, and hydrology have been reported. An up-to-date inventory of production and use of material such as pesticides, fertilizers, road salts, and animal manures is being maintained.

In Canada, research directed towards improving the national monitoring programme is being conducted on such aspects as:

(a) Exploration of new methods and techniques to record data automatically;

(b) Improvements on the quality of data collected;

(c) Employing more sophisticated systems such as earth satellites to transmit data from remote areas; and

(d) Determination of optimum sampling frequency to establish the true picture of water quality.

Another innovation is the collection of background data on water use and the formation of a statistical data base for forecasting water demand.

CZECHOSLOVAKIA

State statistical surveys on water conservation activities come under the competence of the statistics sector of the water economy. These statistics are based on State records. They ensure especially as one of their main tasks the control of the State plan fulfilment. The data investigated in the records are drawn from current registries, accounting files, etc. Additional tasks in the area of water economy statistics are the provision of objective data for managing the water economy to ensure a balance between water needs and the capacity of water resources.

State statistical surveys reflect the directions of principal water conservation activities, as well as the evolution of the organizational structure and the professional water conservation specialization. They are thus classified as inquiries into the waterways' sector and the sector of water supply and the sewage disposal system.

With regard to water supply and sewage disposal, the enterprises of the Water Supply and the Sewage Disposal System are directly managed by regional national committees which are the competent specialized water conservation organizations. The Ministries of Forestry and Water Conservation (MFWC) of both Republics regulate the operation of these organizations in a methodological way. They organize the operation of supplying drinking water from public water mains, and the disposal of waste and rain waters and their purification. The territorial domain of these enterprises corresponds to the administrative jurisdictions of the country.

By means of State records with annual periodicity data are collected
inter alia on the total supplies of surface water including those subject to
payment. The supplies of surface water subject to payment, recorded in
thousands of cubic metres and in thousands of koruna, are classified as
follows: (a) for production of drinking water (i.e. public water mains):
(b) for agriculture including irrigation; (c) industry and other uses,
e.g. cooling. Also recorded are the quantity of waste water discharged into
streams and payments for this discharge. Apart from the total volume of waste
water, there is also recorded the quantity of purified waste water per device
of satisfactory efficiency.

Among these indicators is recorded the pollution produced and discharged
by water conservation organizations (from the public sewage system). Apart
from the total data, the so-called large polluting sources are also recorded
(i.e. those discharging annually more than 200 tons BOD, 200 tons of insoluble
substances, and 300 tons of COD by the dichromate method.

Departmental annual records cover, in the enterprises of the drainage
area (within the Czech Socialist Republic only), the number of pollution
sources and the quantity of pollution in tons per year by most important
departments. For agriculture are recorded pollution from mineral oils,
dissolved inorganic salts and substances increasing water alkalinity or
acidity. Another departmental quarterly record keeps track of payments for
discharging polluted waste waters within the Czech Socialist Republic. With
regard to water mains and the sewerage system, data are collected - in the
State annual record - of water conservation organizations - enterprises of the
water mains and sewerage system - managed by regional national committees.

Investments for the protection of water are recorded by statistical
bodies using a uniform methodology issued in co-operation with the State
Planning Commission. The individual facilities for water protection are
individually recorded in the State statistics of capital investment when their
budget costs exceed 2 million koruna. Individual actions to improve the
present situation and other investment or sanitation measures made on the
basis of particular methodological instructions of the State planning
Commission are also recorded. Direct investors in ecological facilities are
the basic reporting units for the investigations.

Also recorded are the separate facilities for water protection, namely
the self-contained sewage disposal plants and similar facilities to reduce
water pollution, i.e. the construction and enlargement of all existing urban
sewage disposal plants as well as new construction of all sorts including
facilities primarily intended to reduce the pollution discharged and its
influence on flows (e.g. retention tanks and storage reservoirs with
controlled discharge of waste water, phenol-off devices, devices to
concentrate sludges; evaporators), construction or completion of sludge
handling as far as it is part of the technological process of waste water
purification; the construction or enlargement of sludge beds and other
facilities; other investment measures to reduce water pollution, i.e. the
closed-circuit systems of temporary technological use serving as a provisional
arrangement until final solutions can be arranged; changes in production
technologies and processes of an investment character intended, above all, to
reduce run-off significantly and to improve the quality of waste water;
investment actions destined to protect ground-water sources from polluting

activities or installations such as pipelines, refinery pipelines, stocks of propellents and similar devices of chemical plants; as well as other measures of an investment character.

Each facility for water protection records:

- Basic data on construction (i.e. identification data expressed in numerical codes registering the number, stage, character, destination, real term of starting, planned and actual term of take-over by the investor, stage of realization of the facility, budget costs including building costs;

- Basic data on the course of construction (i.e. investment work and deliveries carried out, tangible capital assets obtained for construction; both these indicators record the actual situation from the beginning of construction to the end of the most recent year; they include the plan for the recorded year and the reality since 1 January of the recorded year. All three data take into account the indicator: construction work);

- Performance of construction work (i.e. constructon work is recorded by kind and means of performance, classified by supplier's departments);

- Delivery of machinery and equipment (treated similarly to construction work);

- Capacities obtained by capital construction together with planned and real terms of its becoming operational.

To the extent that a given facility belongs among the obligatory tasks of the State plan, the record on the course of construction is forwarded monthly; for other facilities, it applies to budgetary costs above 2 million koruna quarterly.

State statistical bodies in Czechoslovakia carry out special periodic surveys of technical equipment (i.e. infrastructure) of settlements. These surveys have a five year periodicity. In this way detailed information is obtained on the structure, distribution and state of the equipment constituting a significant part of the environment of dwellings in urban as well as rural settlements. The data on infrastructural equipment are recorded by territorial details (e.g. urban district, sometimes even cadastral plot).

The group of facilities "water supply and sewage from settlements" is fully classified in relevant sub-groups broken down by individual facilities, occurrence in the territory (e.g. drinking water sources, filter plants, water mains, sewerage system, sewage disposal plants, etc.).

Indicators recorded for each individual water conservation facility characterize the distribution (location), operative ability and age of the facility, period of modernization, value of fixed assets, number of workers, topography of the territory. However, these data mainly concentrate on indicators of capacity, functional parameters and utilization of the capacities.

The uniform system of socio-economic information gathered in Czechoslovak statistics enables data on water and the water economy to be also drawn from other statistical sectors. For example, the so-called urban statistics and statistics of communes are collected in a uniform way in each district of Czechoslovakia. They comprise information on water quality in relevant communes. These statistics especially provide local and district bodies with prompt data without putting heavy demands on central data processing.

Hygiene services record and evaluate the quality of water, according to hygienic criteria, especially with regard to the impact on health and the way the water will be used. Such a survey determines the biologic, microbiologic, chemical, toxicological, organoleptic and other indicators. Water for irrigation is also under the control of the hygiene services. As for surface water, the control and other field and laboratory examinations are done using sampling techniques only.

Protection of natural medicinal sources and natural mineral table waters comes under the control of the law on the care and protection of people's health and the decree of the Ministry of Health of both Republics on the protection and development of natural medicinal sources and natural spa institutions. The Czech and the Slovak Inspectorates of spa institutions and springs are the executive bodies of the Ministries of Health in each Republic. The organs and organizations are obliged to report the occurrence of natural mineral sources, thermal, gaseous waters and gases to this Inspectorate. This office registers and protects these resources.

Bacteriological analyses are done by the polyclinics of spa organizations, for organizations where these services are not established, analysis is done by the hygiene services. Chemical analyses of water and gas are done by the Research Balneologic Institutes.

In Czechoslovakia several centralized systems for water have recently been created. In addition to specialized information systems, there exists the so-called "Integrated Information System on Territory" (IST). This concept is based upon the integrated collection of data on territory (and thus also on water) and their related automated evaluation. At present water issues are specified in two registers:

(a) Register of water users: Creation of this register is based upon the information subsystem of water users. It includes three sets of data: users of ground water, users of surface water, and information on discharged water. Water up-take from a given source constitutes the element of the first two sets; in the set of information on discharged water, it is the recipient of the discharge. The presumed number of elements in the register is 15,000. At present, 1979 data are available. Planned predictions for the future cover three five-year periods. The actualization of a two-year periodicity has been planned. The place of up-take and the discharge of water is localized by cadastral territory and further special identification data (e.g. by number of hydrological sequence).

(b) Register of water supplies and sewage system: The data have been obtained from statistical surveys of regional enterprises of water supplies and sewage systems by annual periodicity from 1970 to 1975. The set has been actualized, after a four-year break, on the basis of 1978 data. It is planned to update the data every two years in future. In this actualized set, a settlement locality is a reporting unit, the data on towns will be localized, step-by-step, according to so-called urban districts. The total number of elements is about 10,000. This register includes the following groups of indicators: data on water mains, water produced, invoiced water, water distribution lines, sources, pumping stations and reservoirs, data on sewage disposal systems, sewerage networks and pumping stations.

The IST registers and the data of the State plan will have to be built up in such a way as to be able to use the collected data to a greater extent for multi-aspect processing. Also the recording of the quantity and quality of waste water directly within the production technology should be solved along with the recording of the sludge economy and sludge dewatering.

Control of water quality requires the harmonization of different, often contrary demands. Only the systematic evaluation of water quality in a uniform way will enable a fast identification of changes as they arise or explain their causes and the relevant measures to be adopted. To attain this goal, the statistical organs of Czechoslovakia will gradually not only direct their own activity but also regulate and unify departmental reporting systems and the registration of organs responsible for the environment.

Guidelines for the future orientation of water statistics from the environmental point of view will include the necessity of covering the information requirements of international organizations.

DENMARK

All permit holders are required to measure their annual consumption and report thereon to the appropriate county authority where total consumption is registered, but not always published. In the period 1976 to 1977 the National Agency of Environmental Protection collected and published water consumption data from county water authorities.

In addition to measuring consumption, permit holders are required to analyse the quality of the water abstracted. The requirements as to analysis vary with the purpose of use. As a rule, samples are taken by ground-water drillings for determination of the content of the salts most commonly found in water. The resultant data are collected centrally at the data base of the Geological Service of Denmark (GSD). The most significant data on water quality are obtained through the control of drinking water which is carried out on a continuous basis at the 4,000 waterworks in Denmark. These data are collected by district water authorities. So far, such data have not been collected at a central level.

Nevertheless a private association of operators of major water works (Dansk Vandteknisk Forening) makes an annual collection of waterworks data and publishes them as Water Supply Statistics. In addition to data on the quality of water from waterworks, these statistics comprise data on production and consumption of water, technical installation and power consumption, and on administrative and economic aspects. A detailed breakdown of statistical tables on production and water consumption, on technical systems and energy consumption and on water treatment and water quality is given in annex I.

A first step in the preparation of country-wide statistical surveys is being taken in Denmark where the national Agency of Environmental Protection will make a decision in the near future as to the selection of water data or coverage under a scheme for compulsory reporting to a central authority. A catalogue of water data is being compiled. This catalogue will indicate what relevant water data are available, where these data are stored and how they can be obtained.

FINLAND

Statistics on public water supply and sewerage systems comprise all water and sewage works serving 200 people and more. The questionnaire used since 1970 has remained almost the same and is answered partly by municipalities, partly by the water district offices. Although the data obtained are reliable and directly comparable thus permitting the establishment of time series, their utilization is considered difficult because the system is not yet computerized. Advanced data processing (tests started in 1984) would enable, for example, combined utilization with water quality registers. The questionnaire used so far will be improved, so that only the information which includes changes from one year to the next will be inserted, the rest will be completed automatically. Data on quality of water supplied is collected annually but published at three-year intervals. Sampling is being carried out by water research laboratories approved by the National Board of Health. A detailed list of statistics on water supply, sewerage systems and water quality in water utilities is given in the first part of annex II.

In order to follow up water supply for industry, along with their effluent discharges and water pollution control measures, the National Board of Waters has published every two years since 1972 statistics on industrial water use, water and effluent treatment and relevant investments as well as changes in the pollution load. A lower limit for factories, to be included in the statistics, has been set at 1,000 to 2,000 m^3 per annum of process water and similar water uses. The data are collected using a questionnaire that is addressed to the industrial plants. Obligatory reporting based on discharge permits is combined with the collection of data for industrial water statistics. Obligatory reporting covers 96 to 98 per cent of the total amount of industrial effluents. A detailed list of industrial water statistics is given in the second part of annex II.

Water-use data do not include closed water cycles or reuse of water. Information on raw water quality is also somewhat scattered. Discharges of heavy metals, oils and phenols are often incidental, especially in smaller industries where monitoring and reporting is deficient. As to biochemical oxygen demand (BOD) and nutrient discharges, the coverage of the statistics is very good except for fish farming where plants not answering the questionnaire represent about one-third of the country's production of farmed fish.

Difficulties have also been met in classifying waste-water treatment plants into a limited number of main types. Treatment methods must be viewed in the context of the industrial branch concerned. For example, neutralization may in the metal industry mean precipitation of metals i.e. chemical treatment. Lagooning represents mechanical treatment in the pulp and paper industry and in the mining industry but in relation to food-processing it may represent biological treatment. In-plant water pollution control measures have not been clearly defined. Often measures that

reduce pollution discharge are so closely linked with the production process
that the share of pure water pollution control measures is difficult to assess.

Capital and operating costs of municipal waterworks and sewerage systems
as well as revenues from charges and fees are included in the statistics on
public water supply and sewerage systems. Industry's investments in water
supply and effluent treatment monitoring costs and effluent charges as well as
compensations and indemnities for water pollution form part of the industrial
water statistics.

Together with statistics on sea and freshwater fisheries and on
professional and non-professional fishing, statistics on fish farming are
published annually. They contain more production-oriented information, such
as capacities and value of production than figures on water used and
discharged in terms of quantity and quality.

As the various registers in Finland have been planned and compiled
independently of each other, codes for the same station often differ in
separate registers and files. Common, standardized identification codes for
all water data in the National Board of Waters need to be created. These
codes should apply universally to all registers and files. In addition there
is a need to develop new registers for other important information such as
physiographical data and waste-water load. So far such data are quite
scattered in various manual files and research reports. Resolution of the
question of how to organize a comprehensive register depends, however, on time
and especially on cost/benefit considerations.

FEDERAL REPUBLIC OF GERMANY

Data on water abstraction, water use and discharge are available from the
domestic and industrial sectors as well as from thermal power production
sectors on a regular basis. A breakdown is given in annex III showing
water-use statistics according to supply and waste water treatment in the
domestic and industrial sectors, including mining, manufacturing and thermal
power production. Data on water use in irrigation are collected at irregular
intervals. Self-supply of private households and other economic sectors is
neglected in the water statistics coverage because of its small share of the
total water requirement. Statistics in the sector "Public water supply"
(which primarily meets the water demand of private households, small
industries and the tertiary sector) are broken down according to the following
categories of water resources where the water is abstracted from: ground
water; spring water; rivers and streams; lakes or reservoirs; bank
infiltration, and ground water enriched by surface water. Bank filtration is
water that percolates from rivers or lakes into nearby water abstraction,
mixing with ground water in situ; its quality depends closely on that of its
origins, particularly regarding temperature, odour, taste, and/or chemical and
bacteriological characteristics. Ground water enriched by surface water is
ground water that is artificially recharged. When no distinction can be made
among natural ground water, bank filtrate and ground water artificially
recharged, ground water abstracted falls under the rubrique ground water
enriched by surface water. For economic sectors other than "public water
supply", the last mentioned four groupings are aggregated to "surface water"
showing bank infiltration as a subdivision. This information is completed by
deliveries between the waterworks. Data on water use and discharge can be
obtained from the following surveys:

(a) Survey on public water supply and waste water removal: statistical collection began in 1957 with a survey carried out once every six years, since 1975 a survey has been taken once every four years. The questionnaires are sent to the institutions for municipal water supply, private enterprises and other companies operating waterworks for the public water supply;

(b) Survey on water supply and waste water removal in industry: since 1955, a survey on industrial water withdrawal, use of water and waste water treatment has been conducted every two years. The reporting units are mining and industry establishments having 10 or more employees; since 1977, the size of the reporting unit has been changed to establishments with 20 or more employees. The latest survey refers to the year 1981;

(c) Survey on water supply and waste water removal from thermal power plants: respondants to this survey, which started in 1975, at two-year intervals, are thermal power plants for public supply. The questions correspond to those of the industrial survey.

The survey on public water supply provides not only data on the volume of water supplied to final users, but also data on the quality of water abstracted by public water suppliers. The various techniques for upgrading raw water are classified as follows: (a) treatment for reducing the content of iron, manganese and carbon dioxyde; (b) natural upgrading processes (artificial enrichment of ground water, bank infiltration, sand filtering) and (c) advanced physical and chemical processes. Data concerning the quality of water supplied to the end-users (drinking water) are also recorded. The following parameters, among others, serve as quality indicators: pH; conductivity; content of Ca-ions, Mg-ions, chloride, nitrate, sulphate and phosphate as well as $KMnO_4$ consumption. The amount of water supplied is broken down by communities specifying also the amount supplied (a) lacking drinking water quality; (b) on day of highest consumption; and (c) to households, to enterprises (manufacturing, trade, transport and services) and to other water users including agricultural enterprises, hospitals, schools, administration, fire-fighting, street sweeping, sewerage rinsing, public fountains and parks, baths and toilets. Additionally the number of population supplied is given.

Substantial information on water use can be derived from the statistics for industry and thermal power plants. The input volume is broken down into (a) water for single use; (b) water for multiple use, and (c) water for use in closed industrial circuits. In addition, returns of unused water to the resources and deliveries of water to other firms are covered. The volume of water used is classified into: (a) water for cooling in production processes and in hydroelectric power production; (b) make-up water and (c) water for other industrial processes, which includes, _inter alia_, water used for the generation of process steam, water as a transport medium, water embodied in the products, and water used for sanitary purposes. Special emphasis is given to both multiple use and water use in closed circuits, as efficient water saving techniques. In the initial phase of the surveys, however, some establishments faced difficulties in providing figures on (a) the volume of water contained in the closed circuit and/or (b) the number of turnovers per time unit. Based on these data, the gross volume of water demand (a theoretical figure assuming that no low/non-waste technologies were practised) and a usage factor as the proportion of total demand and water supply can be calculated. At present, the various data on water use are broken down by 34 user categories. For the most important industries, a more detailed classification is possible.

The surveys on waste water treatment and discharge in the Federal Republic of Germany cover data on the following topics:

(a) Collection of waste water: includes detailed information concerning municipalities operating public sewage systems, technical data of these systems and the volume of waste water generated in the municipality broken down by origin (private households and industry);

(b) Waste water treatment: covers the treatment of waste water in public sewage plants as well as industrial installations. For classification purposes, the treatment methods are distinguished as follows: mechanical and chemical treatment as well as biological treatment with and without additional processes. The treatment plants report the volume of waste water treated and the quantity of given substances removed. The noxiousness of waste water before and after treatment is given, both as averaged concentrations and load of: volume of settleable solid (litres); weight (kg) of COD, BOD and cadmium; the latter only for selected economic branches. From this, it is possible to calculate the purification efficiency of the treatment plants;

(c) Waste water discharge: the volume of water returns to the ambient media can be split up into unused water, mainly mining water, and the large portion of water used which includes cooling water and waste water. Such discharges are recorded by the public sewage systems, public treatment plants, industries and public thermal power plants. The total volume passing through the public system is broken down by origin, i.e. private households and commercial enterprises, though in some cases, these are rough estimates only. Data obtained from industry show the flows of used water to the public treatment plants as well as the direct returns to surface water courses. By linking the information from the different sources, a relatively detailed picture of waste water generation and discharge can be obtained; and

(d) Sludge treatment and disposal: information distinguishes the type of sludge treatment: stabilization (anaerobic, aerobic, composting, chemical treatment), thickening, dewatering by means of drying beds, centrifuges, belt and filter press, etc., and disinfection such as pasteurization and radiation. The ratio of chemical compounds applied for sludge conditioning to dry matter content of sludge is also included. Data on sludge disposal are given by volume, percentage and weight of dry matter content for the following disposal alternatives: controlled landfill including enterprise owned disposal sites: agricultural application and recultivation; composting; incineration; and other options including toxic waste disposal facilities.

Quality characteristics of waste-water discharged complete the set of information. Operators of public sewerage systems or purification plants as well as establishments of mining, industry and thermal power plants have been asked to provide data on the amount of suspended solids; chemical oxygen demand, and biochemical oxygen demand discharged. The data reported relate to the total load per year and are collected every four years in the public sector and every two years in the industry sector.

Official statistics comprise additional data on various aspects of water supply, waste water use and waste water treatment, i.e.: economic data (employees, wages, investment, cost structure) in the sector "public water supply"; water prices; investment of industry in installations for waste water treatment and discharge; and data on treatment and disposal of sludge in the public and industrial sectors.

In looking ahead and with a view to improving further water statistics, experts of the Federal Republic of Germany suggest that existing data collection systems and related investigations should be carefully examined to determine the possibilities of reducing expenditures in some areas. For example, it should be determined whether the structures of water resources and sewage management vary enough from one investigation period to the next to justify full investigation each time or whether a random sample investigation would be sufficient. Attention should also be paid to other problem areas, such as the definition of noxiousness or the indices for raw and clean water since they are subject to a certain degree of change owing to improvements in measurement methods or to the enforcement of new laws or regulations.

HUNGARY

The statistics compiled by the National Water Authority (NWA) consist of two groups: so-called functional statistics and special branch statistics. The former contain data mainly on the organization of water management; the latter relate to activities in the special branches of water management. Water use and water quality statistics belong to the second group. The questionnaires used in the data collection process are set out in the first part of Annex IV.

Water demand of households, public baths and institutions is met by the public water supply operated by water management enterprises. Data are, in principle, reported annually by every enterprise producing and supplying water for these purposes for every respective settlement.

Data on industrial water use have been collected by the Central Statistical Office (CSO), the NWA and the Ministry of Industry. The CSO collects data on fresh water use according to standard formats for industrial statistics. Every fifth year, a full survey is performed. A representative survey is carried out every other year. The following data are contained therein: fresh water purchasing according to sources of supply; water usage according to purposes and technology, water recycling, and the quantity of used water, waste water discharge. The representative sampling covers up to 85 to 90 per cent of fresh water use.

Data on irrigation water supply and use as well as on fish farming are collected by the CSO, the NWA and the Ministry of Food and Agriculture at various intervals. There is a special statistical survey for agricultural water use containing questions on main water production works, transport and supplementary information. Another questionnaire asks for data on agricultural water management and water damage prevention. Water production and purchase - separate to that of irrigation water - of large-scale farms are surveyed as well. However, water use by farms e.g. stock breeding, is not dealt with in detail.

Water use in other sectors of the national economy has not been regularly surveyed, and if at all, only at the suppliers' end: water purchase by sectors and sub-sectors are calculated on the basis of accounts. This is particularly true for the use of thermal waters which are considerably utilized in Hungary for geothermal energy production and for medical purposes. So far, only the CSO has collected data on all thermal wells. Within agricultural water use the quantity of purchased and produced thermal water is recorded. The NWA only has information on thermal water production under water management. It has collected data on the quantity of thermal waters with a temperature exceeding 30°C at the outlet. The NWA is going to collect data on thermal water production using a special statistical survey.

Information on water abstraction is collected not only in statistical forms, but also by telex and radio. Data on drinking water production of the producers belonging to the water management organization are delivered to the assigned institute every day in order to compile the total production. Data on the production of industrial water are sent in every week, the quantity of irrigation, thermal and medicinal water produced by enterprises belonging to the water management are collected every month. A detailed presentation of components contained in the Hungarian system of water-use statistics is given in annex IV together with a scheme displaying the collection, storage and processing of water use data.

Although the present system of water-use statistics was in general considered to be quite disaggregated and comprehensive, some problems and limitations relating to the data collected and to the forms used were noted, as follows:

(a) Water uses have been classified from the viewpoint of water and data-suppliers and not according to the actual uses; for example, water quantity used by agriculture, the population and for industrial activities is registered simply as water use for agriculture and domestic purposes;

(b) Statistics on water use contain both measured and estimated data; in particular discrepancies occur when water producers and users do not belong to the water management organization;

(c) Separation of thermal water use causes some problems because users from different sectors can use the same water consecutively (e.g. space heating of institutions, flats, then swimming pools);

(d) Surveys covering water users of all sectors for the same period have not been carried out yet. Various sectors have been surveyed at different intervals.

Data on waste-water discharged are collected by the National Water Authority for the whole country. They are contained in two statistical surveys: (a) the statistical survey for the pollution discharged into the public sewerage network and (b) the statistical survey for the pollution of water. The statistical questionnaires are filled in by water management enterprises operating the public sewerage systems and sewage treatment plants and/or by country authorities. More details on the disaggregated components of these waste-water statistics are given in part two of annex IV.

In 1981, data were collected from 9,200 sewage analyses and 860 significant waste-water emitters. About 15 parameters depending on the characteristics of the observed waste water were measured per analysis. As a result, about 130,000 data are available. Data flow and data processing are the same as in the case of water use (see annex IV).

After analysing the results of the surveys in this field, it may be found that the quality of waste water fluctuates over such a large range that the sampling system used at present does not give reliable results. Because of the inaccurate determination of the quantity of discharged pollutant, the balances of pollutants discharged are not realistic. Inaccuracy may be so great that it may not even be possible to state the direction of changes in the case of the country balance. With a view to improving the significance of such statistics, a new methodological approach has been found to identify more accurately trends and changes in pollutant load discharged (COD, total dissolved solids, ammonium, extractable substances). This methodology is based on the assumption that investments for pollution abatement result in a proportional decrease of pollutants discharged. Together with traditional survey methods, quality changes in effluents will be determined by surveys on water protection investments. To this effect, special guidelines have been issued for the period 1981 to 1985.

Apart from special sector statistics and waste-water statistics, district water authorities collect data in functional statistics, regarding: establishments for waste-water purification and sewerage; plant water management; waste-water use and disposal; and other establishments controlling water quality.

Those engaged in devising and operating data collection systems on the use of water in Hungary are of the opinion that any working method adopted must offer a - perhaps even considerable - degree of flexibility which, while remaining within the framework of the basic postulates enables certain (re-)adjustments to cover also unforeseen future developments.

The statistical information system on the use and quality of water is thus subject to repeated revisions to keep it aligned with current socio-economic changes. Continuity is to be ensured through comprehensive standardization of the terms of reference, consistent with both the nationwide statistical system of other economic sectors and international nomenclature. To promote this task, in 1986 the National Water Authority is publishing the updated version of the manual Standard Classification of Statistical Terms in Water Management, which sets out principles and guidelines for international classification recommended by the Conference of European Statisticians in 1982.

Heightened sensitivity to the various water-related problems has characterized many, if not all, economic and social processes. It was in this context that the Hungarian Act on the Rational Use of the Water and the Protection of Water Quality was promulgated in 1983. Together with the Action Plan worked out for its implementation, the Act provides a sound basis for the efficient and co-ordinated implementation of policy. The Action Plan requires modification of present water statistics, in order:

(a) To yield data on yearly consumption in the various sectors of the national economy;

(b) To monitor domestic water consumption and its sources,

(c) To assess the various water losses,

(d) To provide information on the ecological effects of waste-water discharges and the quality of transboundary waters; and

(e) To analyse the costs of the related services.

Modernization of the communication subsystem of statistical information remains among the priority tasks of water management in Hungary. Accordingly, the National Water Authority has launched a programme to develop a computer-based data acquisition system on water resources, water consumption and users of water resources.

ITALY

Up to a few years ago data available in Italy on industrial water requirements were largely incomplete and fragmentary and so no comparative studies could be made of the sector. A great need was therefore felt to fill this information gap in order to prepare organic plans for water-resources exploitation which would ensure both the efficient use of existing sources while guaranteeing that the requirements of future industrial installations could also be met.

These data were considered all the more important with reference to very arid areas. For instance, the south of Italy has undergone in recent years remarkable industrial expansion characterized by industrial locations often being selected without any careful on-the-spot checks as to the availability of local fresh water resources.

The Water Research Institute of the Italian National Research Council has therefore carried out a number of nationwide and local basin surveys of water supplies available to industry. These studies were carried out in several stages between 1970 and 1980 by sampling a representative number of production units in the various water-using industrial sectors. Data collection was carried out in co-operation with major govermental and private agencies interested in the problem of water supply for industry.

Two main guidelines were followed in carrying out the surveys. The first of these afforded a sufficiently reliable evaluation to be made of water usage for industrial purposes in Italy. At the same time it provided useful data for the fine adjustment of the survey methodology. The second guideline was followed essentially to check the validity of the results obtained and thus increase their reliability. Data were also collected on other production sectors where existing data were not considered sufficient for a correct evaluation of the sample size or specific requirements.

Nationwide and local sampling surveys were carried out seeking the direct co-operation of the representatives of the industrial categories through their response to a questionnaire. Assurance was given that the information so communicated would be rendered available only in aggregated form. This undertaking, combined with the simple and clear way the questionnaire was formulated, assured the high response-rate achieved. This does not mean that the questionnaire could not be further improved, particularly with regard to an accurate identification of products and the way the input water is used. Information was requested on: main production types and annual output; supply sources; location of effluent discharge; treatment of input and effluent water; flow-rates of water used, i.e. input water, total water used, water recycled with or without treatment, water discharged.

For a clear understanding of the survey results, the elements used in setting up the questionnaire are given together with a simplified diagram showing the significance and use of the various flow rates (Figure 1).

Data collected during the surveys yielded a sufficiently reliable picture of the Italian situation pertaining to water supply for industrial purposes. Furthermore, a data collection methodology was developed which may be of use in subsequent surveys of various industrial sectors and individual territorial units, also of "district" size. Processing of questionnaire data allowed the following to be determined:

- Water demand in terms of annual cumulative amount and maximum instantaneous value;

- Water requirements per unit output and per employee;

- Percentage recycling of specific total water requirements in the production process;

- Actual consumption, including losses, evaporation, utilization in the product;

- Percentage of brackish and sea water used;

- Water supply sources;

- Final receiving body of discharge water;

- Probable future trends in water demand.

Special attention was paid to sectors considered significant in view of their substantial water demands. In some production sectors such as the food, chemical, engineering and textile industries, the non-homogeneous nature of the units of measure in which yearly output is indicated, the wide range of finished products and the absence in some cases of any official figures regarding output quantity, often made it impossible to evaluate the size of the production unit sample with accuracy. In any event, the samples comprise a sufficient number of large, medium- and small-sized plants for which a detailed and representative evaluation of the water supply situation was possible. Some difficulty was encountered in processing the data used to determine specific water usage parameters. By and large this was owing to the heterogeneity of industrial production and occasionally also to inaccurate data about destination and use of water inside the plant. The possibility of error in water-balance evaluation was eliminated or drastically reduced by systematically discussing the results of the survey with the collaborating agencies, particularly the industrial associations. This was done to check that the balances tallied with the output and the number of employees.

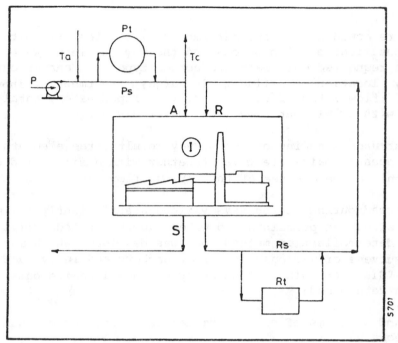

Fig. 1 Circuit diagram showing the various stages of
industrial water usage

P = Water withdrawn: quantity of water withdrawn by the user directly from
the water body.

Pt = Quantity of treated water withdrawn.

Ps = Quantity of untreated water withdrawn.

Ta = Water purchased by third parties.

Tc = Water transferred to third parties.

A = Input water: quantity of water withdrawn which, after any preliminary
treatment, is used to satisfy individual requirements.

I = Total water used: total quantity of water used to satisfy each single
requirement.

R = Recycled water: quantity of recycled water in each single utilization
after recovery at the end of each utilization, with or without treatment.
This includes water in a series of uses.

Rt = Quantity of water recovered and subjected to various kinds of treatment
substantially modifying its characteristics, e.g. heat treatment
(e.g. evaporation towers), chemical treatment (sweeteners) or mechanical
treatment (e.g. clarifiers).

Rs = Quantity of water reutilized without any substantial change in quality
(e.g. recycling of clear water, cascade utilization, etc.).

S = Discharged water: quantity of water discharged, with or without
treatment, into the receiving water body.

I = Factory.

For the purpose of determining specific intake requirements, it was deemed necessary to distinguish between plants using only freshwater and plants fed with both fresh and sea water. Water-utilization criteria referring to plants using sea water differ considerably from those using both sea water and fresh water. Obviously, in the overall economics of water supply for industrial purposes, the use of sea water, whenever the process permits, affords appreciable savings in specific fresh water requirements. This factor could conceivably be taken into account when siting future industrial installations.

With regard to unit water requirements expressed in terms of output, for the purpose of evaluating industrial water demand, it should be stressed that although statistics on industrial production are published annually in Italy, they do not cover the full range of industrial activities. More specifically, in the case of sectors characterized by a high degree of fragmentation and dispersal of production plants, e.g. the food, engineering and textile industries, official statistics cover only the economically more significant production. However, figures are available for the number of employees in these sectors. These data are provided by the General National Census of all industrial activities. Carried out at 10-year intervals, this census covers all production sectors; it is extensively broken down into various levels of industrial categories and territorial reference units. A full evaluation of industrial water demand at national, regional and local levels would thus entail the use of unit "per employee" values of water requirements.

For the purpose of investigating water use in industrial units, data were collected on the total quantity of water used in the production process and the recycled volume of water. Several recycling coefficients for fresh water in both industrial plants using only fresh water and plants using fresh and sea water has been determined. Sea water is known to be used mainly without recycling or, if so, in series. For the various production sectors, these coefficients show the ratio of total quantity of water used to total quantity of water supplied. These coefficients, and the unit water requirements described above, allow mean specific water requirements to be determined for each production sector.

It must be emphasized that data collection on fresh water consumption represents estimated rather than measured values. Whereas meters and pumping capacities could be used to measure water intake and usage, this was not possible in the case of effluent, as discharge pipes are not normally so equipped; thus the figures given have usually been estimated. The significance of the data on actual consumption is thereby reduced.

Nevertheless, the information collected by means of the surveys of water supplies to Italian industry affords a reasonably detailed picture of water usage in the various production sectors. The results of the vast amount of data processed can be considered fairly representative and reliable and may be readily employed to evaluate water requirements for industrial purposes. The same results have already been widely used by the Public Administration and by private organizations to estimate the economic commitments involved in water improvement and protection. Furthermore, at the various stages of the surveys, it was possible to identify the difficulties involved in developing data-collection methods in this field as well as to establish the necessary strategies for further and more exhaustive surveys. Their importance from the standpoint of national resources' planning will depend on the possibility of regularly and periodically updating them so that they continue to reflect developments in industrial structures and production technologies.

POLAND

Responsibility for water management at the country-wide level in Poland is vested in the Department of Environmental Protection and Water Management. The Department determines the distribution of water resources and ensures at the appropriate level surveillance of their allocation and protection against pollution. Before 1960, there were no official statistics in Poland in this field and hence no official publications. After the Central Board had been operating for about 10 years, the lack of such material began to be keenly felt, particularly when attempting to formulate regular long-term plans for the development of the water economy.

Work was thus begun in the early 1970s on the first publication, which appeared in 1975 under the title the Water Economy in the Period 1960-1970. It contained statistical data on: hydrography and meteorology; water resources, abstraction and use; state of water purity, as well as waste-water discharge and treatment; investments and water facilities; costs of maintaining water installations; flood damage; activities of water associations; measuring and monitoring networks; aquatic facilities for sports and tourism; and international comparisons.

To highlight changes occurring in the water economy during a decade, data on the main aspects were given for each year in the form of a synthesis of two five-year periods: 1961 to 1965 and 1966 to 1970. The scarcity of reliable and somewhat comparative data, however, made it impossible to take account of information relating to previous years, so that this first publication of official statistics on water management should be interpreted accordingly.

Emphasis is now being placed on the systematic collection and storage of statistical data, controlling their accumulation, reliability, and processing. Primary information contained in individual reports drawn up by water users is sent directly to the voivode statistical departments. After in situ processing, it is transmitted to the Central Statistical Office for final processing. Occasionally data processed directly by the latter are taken from departmental reports; some relating to water protection are obtained from measurements, monitoring and studies by the environmental protection, State sanitary or hydrometeorological inspectorates. Statistical reports now cover the entire range of water-management questions including materials and costs.

Statistical information on water use - regarding both quantitative and qualitative aspects - is being published periodically in several documents. The statistical Yearbook is the main publication of the Central Statistical Office; it offers detailed data on the social, economic and cultural development of the country, with a considerable portion being devoted to water management. Since 1975 the scope of these statistics was broadened to include waste-water management in the domestic, industrial and agricultural sectors; disaggregated statistical information on waste-water treatment plants is presented along with data on investment, equipment and organization. Relevant elements in the yearbooks on environmental protection and water management are listed in annex V.

Regarding industrial water use and waste-water disposal, it should be noted that surveying is carried out only on industrial enterprises - including thermal power stations - with an annual raw water abstraction of not less than 40,000 m^3. The information on water recycling in industries relates to (a) the extent to which industrial plants are equipped with recycling systems; (b) the ratio of the amount of water in these systems to the total water used in a production process, and (c) the potential amount to be withdrawn from water resources if no recycling had taken place. The indicator for recycling is calculated by dividing the water volume supplied annually for supplementing water losses (irretrievable and in the network) and/or discharges from the closed or semi-closed system, by the amount of water used in the production process. The percentage value of this indicator may range from nil (no recycling) to 100 (theoretical value under conditions of a fully closed system without any additional water supply).

Data on waste-water disposal are being disaggregated according to direct discharge into surface or ground water, discharge into municipal sewer systems, whether subject and subjected to treatment or not. Data on mechanical and biological treatment are being recorded under the heading of biological treatment, while those on mechanical and chemical treatment appear under either biological or chemical, depending on the technology applied. In view of the fact that some factories withdrawing raw water and discharging waste water do not have any measuring equipment or do not carry out measurements often enough, data on such manufacturing facilities are estimated by means of indirect methods, e.g. according to pumping capacity or specific water needs (amount per unit of production).

A considerable part of water-use statistics is devoted to investments and to their material effects in water management, including water protection. Such investments include the following: installations for abstraction from surface water, ground water and mine water together with raw water processing plants and water grids to supply the domestic, industrial and agricultural sector; equipment for collection and treatment of domestic sewage as well as municipal and industrial waste water; river flow regulation and flood control embankments, together with pumping stations outside dikes and in depressions.

Statistics on water management and pollution control are being continuously refined. There is also a trend towards adapting existing publications or issuing specific individual surveys to satisfy the country's internal needs and towards gradually adapting the presentation of data according to progress made at the international level in unifying statistical publications.

Information on use of water in agriculture and forestry collected within the central reporting system pertains to annual consumption of water for irrigation of agricultural and forest land over 20 hectares and refilling of water in fish ponds over 10 hectares. Besides information on water consumption for the above-mentioned purposes and on irrigation methods (e.g. capillary ascent, spray irrigation, flooding, slope irrigation), data on irrigation using sewage are also collected. Moreover, surveys of all agricultural holdings (about 3 million) are periodically conducted. They cover major problems related to water supply for rural areas, i.e. sources of water supply for agricultural holdings (wells, water supply systems, natural springs and the distance between agricultural holdings and the sources of water). In the survey on water supply in rural areas in 1985, the scope of information was expected to have been broadened by the following items: characteristics of water supply systems in rural areas; technical condition of water supply and sewage systems; suitability and quality of water; protected zones around water sources; equipment and exploitation of purification plants operating in rural areas.

Information on water use in agriculture and forestry collected in the central reporting system is supplemented by branch reporting of the Polish Ministry of Agriculture pertaining, inter alia, to irrigation of agricultural land and characteristics of water reservoirs for agriculture.

PORTUGAL

Water statistics are limited to information regarding water supply which are provided monthly to the National Institute of Statistics by local authorities and public water supply works. The results are published in a monthly statistical bulletin. They comprise the following data for the private sector (domestic water use, non-profit making private institutions), enterprises and the public sector (state, local administration, social security): total number of water meters installed; total water supply; supply free-of-charge; charged supply; rent of water meters; taxes and other income. In addition, data is published annually, together with industrial statistics on water use of settlements with piped water supply systems and on the water use of some main cities and important communes. While the above-mentioned data had been collected since 1940, they have only been published since 1970. Data on water use in major cities and important communes has been published since 1978. Relevant data for 1980 are in the process of being published.

Systematic quality monitoring of drinking water is being carried out by local authorities and water-supply enterprises on the basis of the World Health Organization Standards for Drinking Water. Results of these analyses, however, have not yet been statistically analysed.

The department of surveys and planning within the Ministry of Quality of Life is now responsible for setting up statistical indicators and for elaborating ways and means for treating relevant information in a statistical system. To this end, a consultative committee on statistics is to be created within the Ministry.

SPAIN

At present, there exists no statistic published on water-supply use and discharge neither for the domestic and industrial nor for the agricultural sector. The necessary infrastructure for such statistics exists, however: water abstraction and supply is controlled by a permit system; water meters have been installed and waterworks would thus be in a position to record the quantity of water supplied and used by inhabitants, certain industries and municipalities; the quantity of water discharged from reservoirs built by the State as part of the irrigation network is known by the responsible hydrographical services. The water, gas and electricity association, which was dissolved several years ago, had published annual statistical data on the amount supplied by waterworks to cities and communities. With a view to establishing again a system of water-use statistics, the water supply and sewage association has set up a working group to pursue this matter.

SWITZERLAND

Statistics of relevance to the Swiss water economy are extremely diverse as regards their origin, interpretation, coverage and presentation. The possibilities with regard to establishing a co-ordinated system of such statistics are at present limited, a situation which is easily explainable:

(a) Sovereignty over water belongs to the cantons. Planning from the standpoint of water economy, water management and water protection is mostly a cantonal function;

(b) The Swiss federal system is governed by the principle that problems must be resolved at the lowest State level. Thus, solutions to water-economy problems will be sought first of all at the commune or regional level;

(c) With a mean annual rainfall of 1,400 mm and a well-distributed (as regards the concentration of users) network of water courses, few quantitative problems arise in ensuring the rational use of water resources;

(d) Covering an area of 41,293 km^2, Switzerland is one of the smallest countries in Europe. The habitable zone or productive land, in the strict sense of the term, represents only 32 per cent of that area. The wide geographical, climatic and hydrological differences in the country reduce the usefulness of national statistics still further, as the data collected is representative of specific areas only;

(e) In Switzerland, water-economy associations in the private sector are of considerable importance. The statistics established by them occupy an important place in the Swiss system of statistics.

As a result of the above-mentioned factors, the system of water-economy statistics in Switzerland is extremely heterogeneous, but it corresponds to existing needs. The system comprises a mixture of statistics relating to the commune, cantonal and national levels.

At the national level, water-use statistics are primarily the concern of the following bodies: Federal Office for the Water Economy, Federal Office for the Protection of the Environment and the Swiss Company for the Gas and Water Industry (SSIGE). Other statistics, partly confined to particular sectors, are compiled by cantonal offices, federal polytechnic institutes and companies and associations responsible for water distribution and waste-water treatment. The collection and processing of socio-economic data are the responsibility of the Federal Office of Statistics.

As regards future policy, the Federal Commission for studying the apportionment of tasks between the Confederation and the cantons in the field of water economy has decided as follows:

(a) Hydrology: (i) the Confederation shall decide which parameters should be observed at federal and cantonal measuring stations for the various phases of the water cycle and how the results should be used and made available; (ii) the Confederation shall collect, process and make available hydrological data of general interest for Switzerland. It is up to the cantons to collect other data; (iii) the Confederation and the cantons shall bear the costs of their own hydrological activities; observations primarily serving private interests shall be financed by the user;

(b) Water supply: (i) water supply shall remain a matter for cantons and communes; (ii) basic provisions shall enable the Confederation to carry out statistical surveys and to encourage the principal activities of private associations and standards associations. The most important water-economy laws (federal Act on the use of water and hydropower; federal Act on the protection of water against pollution) are now being revised along these lines. Moreover, a new law on statistics is currently under preparation.

As already mentioned, private water-economy associations establish recognized statistics. In particular, SSIGE (see above) has for many years been carrying out regular surveys among its members on the amount of water they abstract and supply to third parties. These statistics cover industrial water supply and water supply to the artisanal sector. Statistically speaking, the term "small-scale artisanal enterprises" denotes artisanal enterprises located in dwellings and whose water consumption is not measured separately and does not exceed 10,000 m^3 a year. Enterprises with their own water supply system are not included in SSIGE statistics.

The purposes of SSIGE surveys are as follows: (a) observation of variations in various water-service parameters; (b) analysis of the current situation and foreseeable developments; (c) bases for establishing the dimensions of water-supply installations; (d) planning criteria for commune, regional and supra-regional projects; (e) means for establishing comparisons between enterprises; (f) comparison of specific parameters with other countries.

The data are collected annually by means of a questionnaire sent out by SSIGE to its members, i.e. water services. A wider survey is made every five years. Today, some 260 services, supplying about 60 per cent of the Swiss population, reply to the questionnaire. The first data were collected in 1901 and related to the operational year 1900. Data are still processed manually. The information obtained is published in a report entitled "Statistical results of water services in Switzerland", which appears annually with a larger issue every five years. The contents are summarized in annex VI.

Since SSIGE surveys do not cover all Swiss water services, it has been necessary to extrapolate from the data obtained to yield an overall picture of the water-supply situation for the whole of Switzerland. Extrapolated values for the entire country and for three categories of water service are also included in the aforementioned publication. These three categories comprise all water services supplying drinking water (a) to fewer than 10,000 inhabitants, (b) to between 10,000 and (c) 50,000 inhabitants and to more than 50,000 inhabitants.

As regards industrial water requirements, the Federal Office for the Protection of the Environment conducts a survey every 10 years or so with a view to promoting the rational use of water, taking the necessary steps to protect and supply water and reducing the quantity of waste water. The information is collected from professional associations, enterprises and SSIGE. The survey is carried out by means of statistical forms. Computerized data processing is planned. The next issue of the publication "The water requirements of Swiss industry" will appear around 1985.

The last industrial survey related to the year 1972 with a questionnaire that filled seven pages. Respondents were asked to complete tables on the characteristics of the enterprise, the nature, quantity, cost and type of water-use and on future water needs. In view of the impossibility of including all enterprises, the survey was confined to those with an annual water consumption exceeding 10,000 m^3. Questionnaires were sent to roughly 3,000 enterprises proposed by professional associations. Only one-fifth of these enterprises (i.e. 600) met the required conditions, that is, only 600 had a minimum annual water consumption of at least 10,000 m^3. This finding afforded additional proof of the dearth of information concerning water consumption in the industrial sector.

The Federal Office for the Protection of the Environment also carries out surveys of the water purification situation in Switzerland. Data are collected from the cantons by means of questionnaires. They are processed manually, but plans are underway to introduce computer processing. The periodical Protection of Swiss waters (first published in 1963) appears at intervals of two to five years, the next issue will appear in 1985. A summary of the contents of two recent reports "Treatment of waste water in Switzerland at the commune level", published in 1979, and "Treatment of waste water and quality of surface water", published in 1983, is contained in annex VI.

Another work dealing with the utilization of additional data obtained by the cantons is already under preparation. It will provide information on waste-water and sludge-treatment plants, the use of sludges and their gases, and water protection in agriculture and industry as well as on aspects of water supply closely linked to water protection.

UKRAINIAN SSR

State recording is applicable to all water resources as well as to water use by industries, transportation, building, agriculture, special enterprises, organizations and institutions regardless of their departmental subordination. Monitoring and recording, keeping water registers, compiling water-management balances and elaborating schemes for the comprehensive use and protection of water resources is pursued at State expense and in accordance with a uniform system. Water-use statistics include data on the amount of water directly withdrawn from water resources, and volume and composition of the effluent discharged into the aquatic environment. Water use is recorded on the basis of the accountability of water users. These data, together with the results from checking the availability and state of equipment and installation for recording water use and discharges, are submitted once a year to the organs of the central statistical control and to those responsible for regulating water use and protection. With the help of computers this statistical information is then processed by economic sectors, districts, large towns, river basins, water-management sections and the Republic as a whole. Compiled water-use statistics facilitate work in the following fields:

- Current and forward planning of water use and the implementation of water-protection measures, as well as the rational development and location of productive forces in the territory of the Republic;

- Development of schemes for the comprehensive use and protection of water, for water-management balances and for keeping the State water register;

- Planning of measures in the field of water management, transport and industry as well as of installations connected with water use;

- Elaboration of measures to improve the efficiency of water-management systems and their operational control;

- Laying down of standards in respect of water consumption and effluent discharges with regard to their quality; and

- Elaboration of measures to prevent or eliminate the harmful effects of waters and other measures to ensure their rational use and protection.

UNION OF SOVIET SOCIALIST REPUBLICS

The necessity for the State to keep statistics on water, water uses and discharges, as well as the procedure for the establishment and processing of statistical reporting are regulated by the Fundamental Water Law of the USSR and Union Republics and by special decisions of the Government of the USSR. The State, co-operative and public enterprises and organizations that use water (housing and communal service organizations, thermal, nuclear and hydro power stations; construction, transport, agricultural and fisheries enterprises; water management organizations operating irrigation and drainage systems and other water management installations; collective farms, State farms and so forth) keep records of the water taken from and returned to water sources using statistical reporting forms issued by the USSR Central Statistical Office.

On the basis of this record, water users prepare statistical reports which they submit to their higher bodies, to the local body for the regulation of water use and protection of the Water Ministry of the USSR, to the epidemiological stations and to the statistical office at the place where the water user is located. In the case of water taken from or discharged into ground-water resources, the report is also submitted to the local office of the geological service. A statistical report on water use is submitted by all water users regardless of the department to which they are attached, the source of the water supply or the recipient of waste water. From this reporting of water users, the Ministry of Water Management of the USSR establishes, with the aid of computers, overall water-use data by Union Republics, river basins and for the country as a whole. These overall data are used in the fields indicated above for the Ukrainian SSR. Details regarding components of this reporting system are given in annex VII.

Altogether, the statistical reporting form contains more than 80 indicators for the provision of information on water use and quality. The specification of water use includes: volume of water abstracted from natural water bodies or obtained from public water supply systems and other enterprises; volume of water used for the domestic and drinking-water needs of the population, production needs, irrigation, etc.; volume of water transferred to other users (unused or after use); and water consumption in water recycling and re-use systems.

The indicators of effluent disposal include the discharge of waste water (clean or polluted or treated in conformity with quality standards in mechanical, physical-chemical and biological treatment installations). This group of indicators also gives the total capacity of treatment plants (mechanical, physical-chemical and biological).

The characteristics of waste water include the composition of the pollutant substances it contains and quantitative indicators regarding these substances (suspended matter, minerals, biological oxygen demand, biochromatic oxidizability, petroleum and petroleum products, fats and oils, phenols, synthetic surface-active substances, heavy metals, salts, sulphates, chlorides and so forth).

Apart from direct data reporting, a number of other economic branches currently carry out surveys which include characteristics of water use and requirements in terms of water quality. The statistical reporting of the epidemiological service, for example, reflects the sanitary condition of water sources for domestic use. The statistical reporting of housing and public services gives information on the extent to which towns and urban-type settlements have water supply and sewerage systems, as well as on the discharge of waste water, including that treated in plants. Capital construction statistical reporting covers the commissioning of treatment installations, irrigation systems, hydrotechnical installations which prevent erosion and runoff, as well as the capital investments in this work. The statistics of the geological service contain information on ground-water consumption by republics, regions and areas. Water intake is calculated, respectively, for the following three groups of ground-water destination: water intended for domestic and drinking purposes, production and process water supply and land irrigation; mineral waters for hospital use; and thermal water for energy purposes and heating.

State recording of water uses in the USSR is a basic source of statistical information on the use and quality of water resources: the data are necessary for: the operational management and control of the use and protection of water resources; forecasting water consumption in agriculture and other branches of the economy; regulating the mutual relations of water users; drawing up schemes for the combined use and protection of water resources; planning and operating reservoirs, irrigation and other water management systems; and conducting research on water management in the country.

UNITED KINGDOM

National data on water abstractions, supply and quality use are collected from Water Authorities and Water Companies by the Department of the Environment (DOE) and the Water Authorities' Association. Annual responses from Water Authorities give average daily abstractions from tidal and non-tidal surface waters and from ground waters according to 10 categories of use and purpose. Water Authorities and Water Companies also report annual figures of average daily supplies of water. Figures of metered water supplies are given for four categories of use. More detailed information is kept by the individual Water Authorities and Water Companies. Statistics of water abstraction, supply and quality and of sewage treatment are published annually by the Department of the Environment in the Digest of Environmental Protection and Water Statistics and its supplementary tables. A breakdown of United Kingdom water-use statistics is presented in annex VIII.

II. STATISTICS FOR POLLUTION CONTROL OF SURFACE AND GROUND WATERS

The survey on ambient water quality statistics carried out on a country-by-country level reveals that in some systems common elements do exist regarding the structure, concept, scope, implementation, presentation and publication, with regard to users and producers. A very rough compilation of main elements illustrating the present situation in various countries is given in annex IX.

It may also be concluded from the information available that, in most ECE countries, more or less elaborated water-quality statistics are kept. They refer, however, almost exclusively to surface water bodies. In only a few cases (e.g. Canada, Denmark, Finland, Sweden, Ukrainian SSR and USSR) do such water quality surveys cover also ground-water resources or estuaries (e.g. United Kingdom).

While in some countries water-quality surveys are carried out and the results kept for internal use by the competent authorities only, water quality statistics are being published in the majority of countries either on an ad hoc basis or at regular intervals, whether months or years. Visual presentation of data on maps showing the quality of surface-water bodies according to a few selected parameters, or according to water-quality classes, is practised in some countries. This aspect had been discussed in the report on comparison and analysis of methods for defining standards of water quality, adopted by the Committee on Water Problems at its thirteenth session (WATER/R.84/Rev.1).

The need to co-ordinate different producers of water-quality statistics - such as water management authorities, statistical offices, non-governmental institutions, federal agencies, local laboratories - has been clearly demonstrated. In a number of recent reports there has been a call for integrating already existing systems into one that is more unified. Concern has been expressed about the disparate nature of data sources as this could create problems of duplication of data production or ignorance of the existence of valuable statistical surveys. There is the further risk that data series or data sets would not be comparable owing, for instance, to the incompatibility of systems, or of their time-frames, units of measurement, definitions, classifications and coverage, for example.

Special attention is being given in a number of countries to the identification of water quality in transboundary waters. Within the framework of, and pursuant to, bilateral and multilateral agreements between riparian countries, such water-quality assessments are to be implemented jointly following commonly agreed methods, including data processing and presentation or else implemented separately in each country at provincial or national levels. Monitored data are compiled jointly by the technical services of neighbouring countries and published by mutual consent. Further information is contained in the proceedings of the Seminar on Co-operation in the Field of Transboundary Waters (Düsseldorf, Federal Republic of Germany, 1984) including the Seminar's report, country monographs, conclusions and recommendations (WATER/SEM.11/3). It is interesting to note the prevailing trend in national systems, whereby the traditional concept of ambient water-quality statistics is changing in a two-fold direction. It has changed:

(a) From an objective resource-oriented approach, which attempted to describe within few classes the quality of surface water according to biological, limnological or other scientific criteria, to a more subjective, use-oriented approach. In the new approach water-quality classification is directly tied to the beneficial uses of particular water bodies by man. As the potential beneficial uses (including those in the domestic, industrial, and agricultural sector, sport and commercial fishing, plant production, recreation and aesthetic elements of the landscape) may be defined differently in various countries, it is to be expected that water-use oriented concepts tend to increase diversification in the national statistical systems of ambient water classification.

(b) From static approach, focusing on the assessment of the state of ground- and surface-water quality, to one which is more dynamic. A kinetic relationship describes better the complex processes of stress-response resulting from the impact of human activities. The dynamic approach, not yet widely applied and still subject to further critical consideration and improvement, attempts to shed light on the transformation of water quality in the whole context of society and environment, using statistical data, among other means. Nevertheless, this concept, too, over-simplifies the complex interactions within the ecosystem and between human activities and the environment. The ecological approach when fully elaborated may become a useful tool not only for "after-the-fact" assessment of aquatic ecosystems but also for signalling an early warning of specific system malfunction - with the help of diagnostic indicators, not yet developed. The ecosystem approach to ambient water-quality statistics seems more suitable for application to spécific ecosystems than for use on the national level as a whole.

The ultimate goal of both concepts is the same. Both resource-oriented and use-oriented concepts of water-quality statistics aim to establish water-quality classes offering a clear-cut presentation and appreciation of statistical data. Almost all ECE countries classify their surface water resources. Quality classes range from three to seven in number. The criteria used to distinguish such classes, however, differ in nature, number and threshold values from one country to another, according to various demands and concepts prevailing at the national or provincial levels.

In some countries, water-quality classes are defined by a vast array of parameters, some 50 to 60 in number, including physical, chemical, biological, radiological, micro-biological and hydrobiological indicators. The array of water-quality variables has made it desirable to strive for a certain compounding of data and to find comprehensive indicators of the state of ambient water quality by means of few quality classes, as a complement to the original and more detailed data. Other countries prefer, for a number of reasons, to use only a few distinct parameters to describe their quality classes. Some countries adhere to the saprobic/trophic system alone or in combination with other parameters. Others base their classification on oxygen demand parameters or on chemical parameters only or in combination with physical parameters. Threshold values of these parameters of quality indicators often differ, even for similar concepts.

AUSTRIA

Unlike the detailed assessment and statistical presentation of all quantitative aspects of the water cycle, carried out by the national hydrographical service, no similar coherent instrument for surveying ambient water quality has yet been developed. Compilation and transfer of data on ambient water quality is divided into several subsectors and branches with different objectives. For administrative purposes, ambient water-quality data are being compiled under the auspices of the Water Quality Surveillance Services, incorporated in the provincial governments (indirectly federal administrations associated with provincial administrations). In addition, relevant data are derived from investigations peridocially carried out on behalf of the Federal Register on Water Management for river-quality classification purposes. At the national level, the Federal Institute for Water Quality is engaged in exploring all factors of ambient water quality. This data source is taken into account in the elaboration of water quality descriptions, such as classification maps.

A great deal of data collection and processing refers to the water quality of the River Danube and other transboundary waters and is being carried out both on a national and provincial level, e.g. on the River Mur, Lake Constance and Lake Neusiedel. Data which are jointly compiled by technical services of riparian countries are published only after mutual consensus has been reached.

While the introduction of electronic data processing for hydrographic statistics is almost completed, only the first steps have been taken in the Federal Institute for Water Quality towards the application of automation. Periodical publications contain statistical information on ambient water quality with a periodicity of five years. They include river quality classification tables for Austria and the federal provinces, a detailed description of river quality shown on classification maps (scale of 1:200,000) and a detailed survey of the federal province concerned. Two examples of statistical publications issued by provinces may be mentioned: (a) Water Quality Atlas for Upper Austria, series published by the governmental authority of the province of Upper Austria; the 1982 issue featured Upper Austrian lakes and their water quality; and (b) the Tyrolean Master Plan on Environmental Protection. The latter can be considered as an inventory of the present situation with regard to, inter alia, ground-water resources, lakes, etc.

Water resources are mainly classified according to biological criteria based on the saprobic system of Kolkwitz-Marsson-Liebmann using four quality classes. According to Austrian experience, no clear-cut and distinct water quality ranges can be found. In addition to biological parameters other values are measured systematically or occasionally, but not integrated into the classification. It therefore cannot be considered a chemical-physical or bacteriological water quality classification. There is no water-quality classification system corresponding to biological criteria, on the one hand, and convertible into chemical parameters, on the other, at least none which can be introduced directly into the quality classification. Doing so would pose considerable difficulties in methodology. Moreover, such a chemical classification of water quality would hardly be meaningful in limiting the indiviudal water-quality classes unless it also considered the main quality requirements, as laid down for various uses.

BELGIUM

A classification of rivers is being carried out in accordance with relevant provisions of the directives of the European Economic Community (EEC), in particular with regard to drinking-water abstraction sites, their determination and classification as well as the determination of bathing quality zones in both fresh waters and sea waters. Minimum standards used in this classification are essentially based on ecological criteria. They take into account specific exigencies of ambient water quality control in Belgium.

Several pollutants and quality parameters are determined systematically in many rivers and particularly in transboundary waters. As compiled for the ambient water quality system, they include: nitrogen, nitrites, nitrates, orthophosphate solubles, total phosphorus, total cyanides, anionic detergents, and heavy metals. Data kept on magnetic tape are published in detail either as tables or maps showing concentrations of various pollutants.

BULGARIA

Surface water is classified according to a system with three categories. These categories are defined with the help of about 60 water-quality parameters or pollution determinants, including biological, biochemical parameters, nutrients, oil, phenols, chemical elements, heavy metals, and radioactive substances. Statistical information is generally not published but utilized by the competent governmental authorities.

BYELORUSSIAN SSR

Surface waters are classified into four categories, taking into account the main water uses. In the first category, water should be suitable for drinking-water abstraction and for water supply to economic activities, including food industries. The second category covers bathing, water sport recreation and those rivers which flow through populated areas. Water quality in the remaining categories should be that suitable for fishing. Category three covers fish breeding of valuable species highly sensitive to oxygen depletion. Distinctions among the four categories are made by means of quality indicators expressed in terms of maximum permissible concentrations of substances of a physical, chemical, biochemical and biological nature, including heavy metals, phenols and anionic detergents.

CANADA

Water quality surveys are conducted on a provincial scale by most of the provinces and on a national scale by the federal Government, with federal monitoring focusing mainly on international and interprovincial boundaries. Such surveys are designed to provide background water-quality data and interpretive information for water resource management and pollution control agencies. The information is considered invaluable in that it identifies both water pollution problems and changing water-quality trends, and indicates whether water quality objectives are being met. The effectiveness of regulatory measures in achieving the desired level of water quality are assessed in this way. It also provides a basis for revising effluent control requirements where necessary.

The need for flexibility and speed in retrieving information in a variety of forms has led to the introduction of computerized data handling systems. The best-known of these systems in Canada is NAQUADAT, the National Water Quality Data Bank. NAQUADAT is designed to store chemical, physical, bacteriological and hydrometric data relevant to water quality for surface waters, as well as ground waters, precipitation, waste waters and sediments. The data base can be interrogated on an interactive basis and information can be retrieved in the form of statistical reports or graphs.

Taking into account the close qualitative interrelationship between surface waters and the respective sediments, Water Survey of Canada had established a sediment network in 1961. It has published relevant data annually or biennially for data from 1947 to date. These data include, inter alia, daily suspended sediment concentrations and load, particle-size distribution as well as bed load.

Difficulties with using current water-quality data for reflecting the critical aspects of ecosystem function were experienced by Statistics Canada, which has recently developed a provisional framework for the Stress Response Environmental Statistical System (STRESS). This integrates information on stress on the environment, including the aquatic environment, resulting from human activities, environmental transformation, social and economic impacts and individual and collective responses. This new concept would require a shift of perspective from the approach of the economist and engineer to that of the ecologist - one that views the aquatic system as not simply a physical-chemical system receiving point source pollution, but a highly complex system integrating stresses of various kinds (thermal discharge, acid rain, shoreline restructuring). Thus, water quality is not considered only from the standpoint of human consumption and industrial use, but also from the point of view of habitat for valued fish stocks and as habitat for recreatonal use. In this context, conventional water-quality data might be modified to reveal other properties of the system (e.g. the dynamics of energy transformation, nutrient cycles, the composition of biota).

The biota themselves serve as a data source for the response side of the aquatic ecosystem. Information is collected both on (a) indicators which refer to sensitive species that are either permitted or excluded by environmental conditions and on (b) integrators which, in this context identify changes in the diversity and composition of the biotic community. This new statistical approach towards ambient water quality assessment had first been tested in the Lower Great Lakes Case Study and is now under review for more general application.

CZECHOSLOVAKIA

State statistical surveys reflect the direction of principal water conservation activities. The surveys also take into account the evolution of the organizational structure and the professional water conservation specialization. They are thus classified as inquiries into the various sectors for rivers and into other branches of water management such as water supply and sewage disposal. Specialized organizations for the operation and utilization of waterways are managed directly by the Ministries of Forestry and Water Conservation of both the Czech and the Slovak Socialist Republics.

The territorial area of these enterprises is based upon the hydrological pattern of the country and follows the borders of drainage areas of main rivers in Czechoslovakia.

With regard to ambient water-quality control, statistical surveys record the length of polluted river sections under the administration of the enterprises of the drainage area which fall within the last two quality classes of a classification of five categories. This classification was not drawn up to reflect the various water uses and their quality requirements but rather for the purpose of comparing different river stretches in terms of water quality, of identifying quality changes in surface waters, as well as for planning and projecting future quality trends on the basis of water-quality control measures applied. The five water-quality classes are defined by means of some 25 indicators including physical, inorganic, organic, micro-biological and hydrobiological parameters.

More use-oriented are the water-quality surveys. These are carried out under the auspices of the Ministry of Health of both Republics, pursuant to the integral function of the hygiene services supervising water supply for drinking water and other purposes, as well as its mode of use. The health services - especially those on the level of districts - concentrate on the quality of water resources used for drinking water purposes, with attention to their conservation and efficient protection. These services also assume responsibility to control the quality of water for recreation and irrigation.

DENMARK

Surveys on ambient water quality have not yet been carried out on a national level. However, local and regional authorities, responsible for regional water-resourse planning, make regular investigations into the state of pollution in Danish watercourses and lakes. Measurements are made, for instance, of nutrient salts and certain bacteria. These statistics are primarily intended for internal administrative use.

At present, the National Agency of Environmental Protection in collaboration with the Geological Survey of Denmark (GSD) and county authorities are planning to establish a countrywide ground-water quality surveillance system. The resultant statistical information will be stored centrally in the electronic data processing facility of GSD.

FINLAND

Ambient water-quality control is exercised on three levels in Finland: the Water Research Institute of the National Water Board assumes responsibility on a national level; the water district office overseas the regional level; and the publicly controlled water-research laboratories take care of the local level. The Water Research Office maintains, in co-operation with the State Computer Centre, a water-quality register and a register of toxic substances. The water-quality register (WQR) contains information on the physical and chemical properties of rivers, lakes, coastal sea areas and aquifers. The toxic substances register (TSR) contains information on toxic or noxious substances in sediments and aquatic organisms. Both registers include not only monitoring data but also information obtained from separate investigations.

One record in these registers (information from one sample taken) consists of data from sampling sites and from the samples themselves. Apart from geographical, administrative, climatic, meteorological and hydrological background information for each record, the following data can be recorded for each sample in the WQR: Secchi disc transparency, sampling depth and maximum depth at the site; as well as codes and the measured values of approximately 150 variables. Additional information kept in the TSR includes reference material and the conditions under which the sample was stored.

The information stored in the registers is retrievable as specific data reports generated in the form of lists, statistical summaries, plots, etc. This can be accomplished by library programmes as well as by a set of programmes developed especially for these registers.

For over 10 years, a five-level water quality classification has been used in Finland for the estimation of surface water quality. This scale was based on a similar classification used in Sweden. In this general classification, natural or nearly natural waters are grouped into the two first categories (excellent and good) suitable for all users requiring good water quality. (For drinking water supply to communities and other similar purposes, only mechanical treatment and disinfection would be needed in the first quality class while chemical treatment was foreseen in the second class; also for fishing purposes and recreation, these categories would comply excellently.) Waters polluted by effluents or impaired by other human activities were assigned to classes III and IV, satisfactory and fair, respectively, with differentiated assignment for various uses such as recreation, cattle feeding, irrigation, cooling, timber floating and hydro-power production. Waters belonging to class V are scarcely suitable for any use and not suitable for one which depends upon good water quality.

The class boundaries were defined on the basis of a limited number of indicators including fecalstreptococci, colour, COD, BOD_7, O_2, toxic substances, heavy metals, oils, floating substances, lignin, iron, manganese and aquatic bloom. If oil, scum, floating waste and/or toxic substances are observed in a certain water area repeatedly and their contents exceed certain threshold values, the water stretch is always classified as belonging to the last two classes despite all their other properties.

As this existing classification system has turned out to be in many respects unsatisfactory, in 1981 the Finnish National Board of Waters entrusted a task force with the development of a quality-based classification of water bodies according to suitability for different uses. Application of this classification should facilitate: (a) detailed planning of water use and pollution control; (b) surveys of ambient water-quality and (c) estimates of both the harmful effects of alterations and the magnitude of the financial compensation entailed by such alterations. A complementary, general classification is intended to provide an estimate of general water quality in watercourses, regions or even for the whole country.

To achieve this aim, separate usability classification criteria are now being developed for the three modes of water use most dependent on water quality, namely: recreation, municipal water supply, and fishing. The recreational classification, tentatively applied since one year, includes six classes. The two best classes contain waters in a natural or almost natural state (without point-source pollution and with little or insignificant non-point source pollution). The third class contains natural waters in which humus or clay occurs in large amounts, those which are highly eutrophic and/or those which are slightly polluted. Classes 4 to 6 include watercourses polluted to increasing degrees by effluents or other agents considerably altering water quality.

The classification is divided into a description of each group and the statement of the threshold values of the variables defining the class boundaries. In the case of humus-containing waters, the relevant variables are: water colour and secchi depth; in the case of eutrophic waters: chlorophyll a, phytoplankton biomass and mean total phosphorus; in the case of pelotrophic waters: turbidity and concentration of suspended solids. Additional variables used if water is polluted are: COD, NaLS concentration, oxygen deficiency, fecal coliform or fecal streptococci, oil or similar substances, and mercury concentrations in carnivorous fish species.

A further sophistication of this classification system pertains to the calculation method, which distinguishes separately whether water is used predominantly for swimming or recreational fishing. A set of instructions has been drawn up for the interpretation of results, taking into account, among others, the character of the water body. After the examination, the recreational utilization number R is defined. This number can then be allocated to one of the six recreational use classes.

Work has now begun in Finland on the second, the raw water classification, comprising five raw water classes. The defining factor has been the extent of the procedures required for water purification. In each class, variables have been defined such that, according to the water-purification method attributed to the group classification concerned, the drinking water obtained would at least meet the quality standards in force. These variables are (a) health associated variables (all toxic compounds, substances deleterious to health, and hygienic indicators); (b) variables affecting odour and taste (ammonium, phenols, mineral oils, species composition of phytoplankton); (c) variables affecting the ease of water purification ($KMnO_4$ - value, colour values, pH, chlordies, sulphates, turbidity, fluorides, iron, manganese, lignin, chlorophyll) and (d) general water-quality variables (temperature, secchi depth, electrical conductivity, oxygen concentration, anionic tensides, total phosphorus).

In the interpretation of results, the greatest emphasis is placed on toxics and other substances deleterious to health, with descending priorities for (b), (c) and (d) above. This classification system developed for surface waters can to some extent be used for ground waters, too. However, a separate five-level water classification for the precious resource is under preparation. Also, the classification on fishing, the most difficult to design, is in the development stage. The most important quality variables will include oxygen concentration, pH, colour value, chlorophyll a and concentrations of toxic substances in fish, for the lowest quality classes. In addition, information on the structure of fish population and the practical facility of fishing will be taken into account.

FRANCE

The idea of preparing inventories of the degree of surface water
pollution in France was given legislative expression in the Act of
16 December 1964. Three five-year inventories were prepared in 1971, 1976 and
1981. The results of the latest inventory were published in 1982. The water
Service of the Pollution Prevention Department of the Ministry of the
Environment has been responsible for co-ordination (a) at the central level
(in the Ministries of Agriculture, Health, Industry and Transport) and (b) at
the regional level (the water basin commissions, with the support of the six
Water Basin Financial Authorities together with various other bodies).

In carrying out these inventories, it was always recognized that the
concept of water quality involves a number of fields (physics, chemistry, and
biology, in particular) and that change of ambient water quality has a direct
impact on various water uses: economic (industrial and agricultural sector);
socio-cultural (recreation, sport, etc.); ecological (capacity for
development and maintaining aquatic life and sustaining life in general) and
last but not least, hygienic (drinking water supply). Some 40 parameters
chosen for the statistical expression of ambient water quality therefore cover
a wide range of disciplines. They are grouped as follows: physical and
oxygen-related parameters, toxic and undesirable elements and compounds,
micropollutants, bacteriological contamination and radioactivity.

Together with these basic data, background information is kept for each
site on the hydrological, administrative, geographical and esthetic nature
(presence of leaves, mud, colour, turbidity, smell, etc.). In 1971, about
220,000 items were stored in files per département, water basin and the entire
country; by 1976, the figure was 350,000. These data are then processed by
computer to detect deviations, which are identified by means of probability
tests. Data found incorrect are rectified and incorporated back into the data
bank. Since 1978, the data processing programmes have been identical for the
six Water Basin Financial Authorities and the Water Service.

The main publications in France are the consolidated reports on the water
quality inventory. Other statistical outputs of these inventories can be
found in the yearbooks published by the Ministry of the Environment, water
quality target maps prepared by the Water Basin Financial Authorities and
départements and in other annual reports on the state of the environment. The
simplest outputs consist of site-by-site presentation of information for each
parameter synchronically (by direct transposition of the data stored in the
file) and diachronically (by regression curves). The results are presented in
the form of distributuion tables for entire sites, either analytically
(parameter-by-parameter) or as consolidated values (by quality class). The
consolidated measurements for various parameters are presented in terms of EEC
quality categories (1A, 1B, 2, 3 and 4). Category 1A denotes water of the
"best" quality suitable for all uses; category 4 means lowest quality.

In addition to tables, cartographic presentation of statistical
information is considered particularly useful to identify regions where a
given critical threshold is exceedeed at a particular percentage of sites.
Thus it draws attention to any deterioration or improvement in the quality of
a water body in respect of a given parameter. There are 23 such analytical

maps, showing the state of pollution for each parameter and subject maps identifying points with low, average or high pollution probability for each group of parameters (organic matter, mineral substances, toxic substances, etc.). Finally, current-state and target maps for water give a consolidated picture by quality category of the degree of pollution in specific river sections. They are prepared by extrapolating from the values obtained at the various sites along a river.

GERMAN DEMOCRATIC REPUBLIC

The Water Board of the German Democratic Republic is in charge of monitoring the quality of flowing and stagnant waters and the observance of the regional limit values. It comes under the Ministry of Environmental Protection and Water Management. Measuring stations to monitor the quality have been established at all important rivers and the most important natural lakes, reservoirs, low-land storage reservoirs and lakes artificially created in exhausted open-cast mines. It should be noted that only parts - so-called sections under investigation - of the total length are selected for monitoring. Such sections are selected predominantly for their significance in terms of water use in the area concerned. Observance of standards for waste water by the industrial and agricultural units located in the section is also monitored. The measuring stations may be fixed at different river sections every year. The observations, however, are carried out year-round. The stagnant waters investigated (lakes, reservoirs, etc.) are selected also in regard to the purpose for which they are used. This is done with a view to their environmental and ecological functions and the possibilities to use them for recreational purposes.

The State Water Board's authorities (water management boards, river boards) determine the water quality on the basis of water use and protection standards. Relevant standards of the German Democratic Republic are:

- TGL 22764 of 1 March 1981 - Classification of Water Quality of Flowing Waters;

- TGL 27885/01 of 30 April 1982 - Stagnant Inland waters Classification.

In accordance with the standards recommended for the member States of the Council for Mutual Economic Assistance (CMEA), new surface-water quality classifications were prepared in the German Democratic Republic from 1981 to 1982. They are used to determine and monitor the possibility to make use or restricted use of waters as a result of their quality, and form the basis for rehabilitation measures. Simultaneously, they can help characterize the investigated river sections or lake areas in ecological terms. The institutions of the State Water Board also undertake to analyse the measuring data as determined. The analysis regards the concrete section of the investigated river or stagnant water in its relation to the respective river area or region. If permissible water-quality limits are exceeded, rehabilitation measures are taken or conditions imposed on the enterprises which caused the pollution, with a view to stimulating purification of their waste water. The State Water Board is also in charge of evaluating the data obtained from the section monitored. Conclusions are drawn regarding the situation in the entire river or region concerned. Where values are found which exceed the fixed limits, the necessary relief measures are taken or the enterprises responsible are charged with the obligation to purify their waste water.

Principles governing classification of water quality of flowing waters in the German Democratic Republic

The quality of flowing waters is classified according to three characteristics: (a) organic load and oxygen balance; (b) salt load; and (c) other harmful substances from land-based sources. Organic load and oxygen balance are criteria used to assess the internal relation in qualitative and quantitative terms. By doing so, the classification serves as both a description of the water quality and a characterization of the water under ecological aspects.

The above-mentioned groups are subdivided into six classes depending on ambient quality. Five of the six classes characterize water quality in regard to its possible use for: drinking water; recreational purposes and fish culture; process water; cooling water; irrigation water in agriculture. Use-class 6 characterizes water which, except for navigation, is not fit for any type of use and is severely harmful to the environment owing to its toxic load and corrosive properties.

Organic load and oxygen balance display a marked annual cycle which depends upon the water's hydrologic conditions, its temperature, biological conditions and the users' behaviour. Classification must be done during the period of the most adverse conditions. That period has a decisive impact on reducing water-use possibilities and affects the rehabilitation measures to be taken. The biochemical oxygen demand which reduces the organic load is the most significant criterion regarding the classification of the water sections under investigation. The biological oxygen demand (BOD_5) must not exceed the following limits:

Use-class 1 (predominantly drinking water)   4 mg O_2/litre,

Use-class 2 (predominantly water for recreational
         purposes and fish culture)   10 mg/O_2/litre,

Use-class 3 (predominantly process water)   20 mg O_2/litre,

Use-class 4 (predominantly cooling water)   40 mg O_2/litre.

Use-class 5 (predominantly irrigation water)   may exceed the above limits

Flowing waters which are severely affected by phytoplankton are analysed separately, i.e. by other criteria.

The salt load of waters mainly depends on the flow. Its absolute quantity depends upon the given geological conditions of the catchment area and industry's waste-water discharges. The total salt content is limited in individual use classes as follows:

Use-class 1   350 mg/litre,

Use-class 2   750 mg/litre,

Use-class 3   1,500 mg/litre,

Use-class 4   2,500 mg/litre,

Use-class 5   4,000 mg/litre.

The salt load is determined by averaging the water's content of calcium, magnesium, sodium, chlorides and sulphates

The concentration of other substances contained in the water is the third water-analysis criterion. Process-related substances contained in the waste water, such as free cyanide, nitrate, fluoride, phenol and heavy metals, determine the classification of the water into one of the use-classes.

The following limits have been fixed with regard to the substances which may be filtered out:

Use-class 1   10 mg/litre,

Use-class 2   20 mg/litre,

Use-class 3   50 mg/litre,

Use-class 4   100 mg/litre,

Use-class 5   200 mg/litre.

The water's use-class depends on the lowest average of any criterion.

The standard concerning the quality classification of flowing waters also imposes comprehensive measures for the protection of waters. Stringent, careful management is planned in relation to water belonging to use-classes 1 and 2, which represent valuable resources for all types of high quality demands. It must be impossible for such waters to be polluted by poisons, toxic waste products and harmful substances. In implementing water engineering works it is to be ensured that the ecological spectrum and balance are maintained in the catchment area.

In regard to use-classes 3 and 4, which are suited for different types of use either without purification or after prepurification, a further loading by poisons or other harmful substances has to be avoided. Comprehensive rehabilitation measures are necessary, especially with regard to waste-water treatment, so that the water quality attains the standard of use-classes 2 and 3 not only at the individual location but generally. Extensive rehabilitation efforts are necessary for the waters belonging to use-classes 5 and 6. Their usability, which is reduced by poisons, toxic wastes and other harmful substances, is to be improved.

Principles governing the classification of the water quality of stagnant
inland waters in the German Democratic Republic

The classification of lakes, reservoirs, low-land storage reservoirs and
lakes artificially created in exhausted open-cast mines is intended to provide
an overall picture of their water quality. Like the quality of flowing
waters, that of inland waters is analysed according to three groups of
characteristics: (a) hydrographic and regional criteria; (b) trophic
criteria; (c) salt content, special and hygienically relevant criteria.

Several criteria are combined in each of these groups to form sets of
characteristics which can be used to assess the water. Potential uses of the
stagnant waters analysed are indicated by the use-classes into which the water
is classified after the three groups of characteristics have been weighted.

Classification by hydrographic and regional criteria follows a three-fold
division: (a) water morphometry; (b) hydrographic relations between the
catchment area and the body of water; (c) anthropogenic load.

Characteristics (a) and (b) describe the natural status of the water;
the anthropogenic load is found using criteria of that which changes the
natural status. The group of hydrographic and regional criteria represents an
expected value which correlates with the group of features characterizing the
water's trophic state.

The classification by trophic criteria includes the biologically
effective criteria which have a bearing on the oxygen balance of stagnant
water. They form the following groups: (a) oxygen balance; (b) nutrient
conditions; (c) bio-productive conditions.

Classes determined on the basis of these groups reflect the water's
trophic condition. If the classification by the latter set of criteria is
into a lower class than by the hydrographic criteria of the preceding set, the
anthropogenic load indicates whether or not the water quality can be improved
by taking measures in the catchment area or in the water body itself.

The third group includes characteristics important with regard to the
potential use of the water: (a) salt content; (b) special criteria; (c)
hygienically relevant criteria. Because of the heterogeneity of these
characteristics, the standard calls for the indication of the chemical symbols
of those important criteria which are decisive for the classification of the
body of water.

Evaluation of the water data obtained

The evaluation of the data obtained for a section of a flowing or
stagnant water body serves to classify water into one of the six use-classes.
To that end, the data obtained is compared to the limits fixed for individual
criteria and use-classes. The data of "typical flowing waters", for example,
are to be determined and anlaysed as follows:

(a) organic load and oxygen balance

Saprobic index - worst (highest) value,

Other criteria - average of two successive worst values in an
annual cycle.

The use-class with regard to the organic load and oxygen balance is
determined by averaging the class values of the individual criteria and
rounding this average to the nearest integer.

(b) Salt content

If samples are available which are evenly distributed over the entire
year, their empirical frequency distribution is to be calculated and the
90 per cent value of the cumultative frequency derived. Each criterion is to
be classified into the respective use-class by comparing the 90 per cent value
of the cumulative frequency to the limits.

(c) Other substances specific to the region concerned

The data are to be analysed in the same way as for salt load. Each
criterion specific to the investigated body of water is to be classified into
the respective use-class by comparing the 90 per cent value of the cumulative
frequency to the limits. The lowest value of a criterion determines the class
into which the water is classified.

Annual evaluation of the results is done using the following data:

- Indication of the location of the measuring station, its function, length
  of section monitored (kilometres);

- Determined criteria of the oxygen balance, ratio of the class values and
  use-class;

- Determined criteria of salt load, ratio of the class values and use class;

- Determined values of region-specific criteria, classification into the
  use-class;

- General use-class of the water at a given location, described by a
  three-digit index (e.g. 132, i.e. oxygen content = use-class 1, salt
  load = use-class 3, and other criteria = use-class 2.

The classification of flowing waters into the use-classes so determined
may be shown in a diagram or depicted cartographically.

In order to classify stagnant waters:

- The hydrographic and morphometric conditions are determined by means of
  depth-mapping of lakes, and

- Use-related loads are entered as permanent data valid for prolonged
  periods of time.

In order to obtain the data for a classification by the characteristics groups of

- trophic criteria

- salt content, special and hygienically relevant criteria,

the measurements are to be carried out as follows:

(a) drinking-water lakes or storage reservoirs: at least ten measurements a year, including monthly measurements from April to October;

(b) all other lakes and storage reservoirs: at least six measurements a year, including four times from April to October.

The general quality-class of a stagnant body of water is calculated as the arithmetic mean derived from the non-rounded class values of the characteristic group rounded off to the nearest integer.

Example for the classification of a stagnant body of water in the German Democratic Republic:

Characteristics group (short description)	Average of the criteria	Characteristics class
(a) morphometry	2.6	
(b) catchment area	1.9	
(c) load	2.7	
Characteristics group by hydrographic and regional criteria	2.4	2
(a) oxygen balance	2.0	
(b) nutrient condition	3.2	
(c) bio-production	3.2	
Characteristics group by trophic criteria	2.8	3
(a) salt content	1.2	
(b) special criteria	2.5	
(c) hygiencially relevant criteria	3.0	
Characteristics group of special criteria	2.2	2
General class	2.5	2

According to the German Democratic Republic classification, stagnant water belonging to use-class 2 may be suited for the following use types:

Use as drinking water:	After normal treatment
Use as process water:	After usual pre-purification
Use as cooling water:	Without any pre-purification
Use as irrigation water in agriculture:	Fully usable
Use for recreational purposes:	Without any restrictions
bathing, navigation and sports yachting:	Inadmissible, if the water is intended for use as drinking water.

With regard to waters belonging to use-classes 3 and 4, the treatment and pre-purification processes are more complicated, and they may be used for recreational purposes to a limited extent only. With the exception of a few purposes, water belonging to use-class 5 is not generally usable, and water belonging to use-class 6 is unusable (except for navigation).

The present aim of improving the statistical presentation of ambient water quality data is to increase the proportion of measurements and to enhance the territorial subdivisions of statistics by including all relevant fields of investigation within an integrated system ready for electronic data processing.

GERMANY, FEDERAL REPUBLIC OF

Water authorities of the federal Länder classify water bodies according to quality following generally agreed systems: for stagnant waters and lakes, the various trophic levels - which reflect water quality - are applied; for flowing waters, quality grades are basically founded on the saprobic system. To make the classification system applicable to all water bodies in the Federal Republic of Germany, the definition of quality grades had to be restricted to generally recognizable criteria reflecting only characteristic organisms and/or their combinations. It was found that in densely populated regions and highly industrialized areas it was almost impossible to assign many chemical parameters to the few, established water-quality classes.

A number of studies carried out recently has shown, however, that correlations exist between biological quality indicators and water chemistry parameters. Therefore, random investigations of ambient water quality based on chemical parameters confirm and support biological findings in many cases.

The classification of stagnant water and lakes falls into four categories, according to trophic conditions: oligotrophic, mesotrophic, eutrophic and polytrophic. For definition of classes, the following indices are used: nutrient content, plankton and phytoplankton production, oxygen concentration and visibility depth, for the most significant water layers of the water body.

Basic assessment of the water quality of flowing water encompasses the gradual differences in their general and biological state in the course of self-purification processes after pollution with organic substances as described by Kolkwitz, Marsson and others, in the so-called saprobic system. The waters are classified into four water-quality classes with intermediate steps in between. The classes are based on biological criteria: typical population of fish, insects, worms, algae, bacteria, fungi, mosses, flowering plants; appearance of sediments and gravel; turbidity. In the definitions of the various quality grades only the biochemical oxygen demand (BOD), ammonium concentration and dissolved oxygen are retained as essential chemical criteria. Hygienic and bacteriological aspects are not taken into account. A full presentation of the classification is given in annex X.

The attempt to describe the complex field of water pollution in a seven-stage quality system must, of course, result in a compromise neglecting a number of natural condtions. The oxygen balance of water courses in mountainous regions, for instance, will react differently from that of lowland waters with equal organic pollution.

Another problem is the proper assessment of toxic substances that lead to a more or less pronounced reduction of aquatic flora and fauna and inhibit self-purification processes. Although these effects cannot be directly attributable to heavy organic pollution load, the water is classified into quality grades III to IV or simply IV of the classification system, in the case of massive toxic pollution. The impact of effluents with high salt content - as far as this will not lead to a considerable reduction of species in the water body - is not covered by this classification system nor is the concentration of toxic substances or resistant organic compounds.

It should also be mentioned that during the process of self-purification, there are no abrupt changes from one stage to the next, but only gradually changing conditions. Therefore, during autopurification the establishment of the point where the water body may be regarded as passing from one quality grade to another is rather fuzzy. As a rule, the quality grades entered in the water quality map should be changed only on the basis of substantial findings. Visual presentation of quality data using coloured maps is considered an efficient tool for a sound orientation and to inform the public-at-large regarding the state of present ambient water quality.

GREECE

Ambient water quality characteristics are surveyed regularly at fixed geographical locations across the country. Generally, the statistical data are not published but remain for internal use by competent authorities. Parameters and indicators of pollution include: BOD_5, COD, suspended solids, heavy metals, phenols, nitrogen, phosphorus, coliform and streptococci counts.

HUNGARY

Exploration and control of water quality is not exclusively a water management activity. Instruments and installations of other sectors - e.g. agriculture or public health - as well as universities, research and planning

institutes play an active role in Hungarian water resources. Hydrochemical
and hydrogeological control is carried out within the network managed by the
water-management authorities. These control measurements cover the measuring
of hydrochemical parameters, saprobiological surveys, algae counts,
"a-chlorophyll" and photosynthesis tests. Data on the quality of surface
waters are recorded by the laboratories of the water-management authorities in
a form suitable for electronic data processing. Every sample is registered as
follows: place and time of sampling, description of the hydrological
conditions and some 52 characteristics of water quality. Entered on a second
sheet in the register are the minimum, maximum and design parameters for 14
special characteristics measured at the same sampling site year round,
together with the quality class of each characteristic. The records are
forwarded to the Scientific Research Institute for Water Management where
processing is carried out by computers after checking. Water quality data are
published in yearbooks.

The methodological basis currently used in Hungary for the analysis of
water quality data is the classification of the quality of surface waters
accepted by CMEA in 1979. It determines an annual indicator of water quality
at 90 per cent durability and compares it to the limit values. The
classification system integrates the characteristics of water quality into the
following four groups: (a) general physical and inorganic chemical (mineral)
characteristics; (b) general organic chemical characteristics; (c)
characteristics of inorganic industrial pollutants; and (d) characteristics
of organic industrial pollutants. To each group of pollutants six
water-quality classes are attributed. They are defined by limit values of the
various parameters. Some 50 parameters are given for the first two groups,
including, among others, oxygen, phenols, detergents, phosphorus, nitrogen,
heavy metals.

Six biological classes are distinguished by the CMEA system on the basis
of the so-called "S" index of saprobity. The trophic condition is evaluated
according to chlorophyll content but in this case the average values measured
during the growth season are compared to the standards.

The analysis and classification of ambient water as part of immission
control does not provide close links between survey data and quality standards
compared to the process of emission control. In the latter case, an item is
classified almost simultaneously with measurement. Several problems arise in
the classification system regarding frequency of sampling and the parameters
observed. The description of the quality of surface waters is made on the
basis of the reported classification system in Hungary, but it cannot be used
in the case of indicators which are not measured, or for which adequate
homogeneous data series are not available.

Maps are generally used for data presentation in Hungary. On the basis
of the indicators analysed, the quality of the more important watercourses for
a given year is represented by stripes of different colour and width, tracing
a stream. The colour code of the six water-quality classes and the meaning of
the different stripes are explained on the maps. The width of the stripes is
proportional to the mean flow of the stream.

NETHERLANDS

Water pollution in surface water bodies is surveyed periodically and on an ad hoc basis by water control boards, provincial authorities, public works departments, and the national water supply institute for public health research. Since 1973, quarterly reports have been produced on the quality of stretches of water bodies under the responsibility of the central Government. Statistical information on other water bodies is published annually in provincial or regional reports.

In the multi-annual programme for 1975 to 1979 to combat surface water pollution in the Netherlands, a national surface-water quality classification has been elaborated by the Ministry for Transport and Public Works. It is based on the oxygen régime of surface waters. The three characteristic parameters are: biochemical oxygen demand (BOD_5^{20}), percentage oxygen saturation and ammonia content. Ammonia is used as an indicator because of its connection with oxygen demand and its value as a biological indicator.

More or less arbitrarily, a division into five water-quality classes was chosen, partly on the basis of experience gained and partly as a result of theoretical research. For each measurement of the three parameters, a code is determined according to the scale in table 1 for a specific site and specific time. Codes derived at different sampling times are weighted and averaged to obtain the water-quality class of a particular sampling point (see table 2).

Table 1

Code No.	% O_2-saturation	BOD_5^{20} (mg/l)	NH_4^+-N (mg/l)
1	91 - 110	≤ 3	< 0.5
2	71 - 90	3.1 - 6.0	0.5 - 1.0
	111 - 120		
3	51 - 70	6.1 - 9.0	1.1 - 2.0
	121 - 130		
4	31 - 50	9.1 - 15.0	2.1 - 5.0
5	<30 and 130	> 15	> 5.0

Table 2

Class	Colour code	Average points
1	blue	3 - 4.5
2	green	4.6 - 7.5
3	yellow	7.6 - 10.5
4	orange	10.6 - 13.5
5	red	13.6 - 15

It should be noted that under completely natural conditions, the criteria of class 1 will generally be satisfied. Surface water meeting minimum provisional standards will be at least of class 3.

This surface water quality concept, whether based on chemical or biological measurements, should be applied only with extreme care, particularly when the quality of the water is subject to regulations essential for bringing a watercourse up to, or keeping it in, a particular condition.

NORWAY

The Ministry of Environment has general responsibility to develop information systems for the plannng and administration of policies for resources and the environment. The practical job of developing and maintaining such information systems was given to the Central Bureau of Statistics (SSB), the primary producer of statistics for most areas where political authorities and others need statistics as a basis for decisions.

In its experimental work on resource accounting, SSB did have an urgent need for the establishment of a register of the various parts of the Norwegian rivers systems; a preliminary register of river sections influenced by hydroelectric development and production was established first. SSB now plans to extend this register to cover the remaining Norwegian river systems, and to link the catchment areas defined by the register to a system of small geographical areas (districts), thereby making it possible to have statistics on populations, buildings and their sanitation systems, agricultural production, etc. of the catchment areas, based on data from the Population Census and the Census of Agriculture and eventually on administrative records. These projects are funded by the Ministries of Environment and of Energy. The Norwegian Water Resources and Electricity Board (NVE) was expected to take over the formal responsibility of the register - being able to utilize the preliminary work of SSB.

In designing this statistical system, it was also recommended that already available information should be used to classify roughly all Norwegian waters into three or four classes according to potential pollution from activities in the catchment areas. Different sampling ratios would be useful in each class - ranging from 100 per cent in the top group (those which "must" be included) to perhaps less than 1 per cent in the group of least-exposed waters.

Ambient water quality data can also be found in the Norwegian compendium of environmental statistics published by the Central Bureau of Statistics. In the section on water quality, selected watercourses or lakes have been described by their physical and chemical parameters: temperature, pH-value, conductivity, colour, turbidity, potassium permanganate, chloride, sulphate, potassium, sodium, iron, manganese, silicum, aluminium, zinc, lead, copper, cadmium. The information on water pollution is mainly reported in composite categories, such as "hardly", "moderately", "substantially", and "heavily" polluted, but a separate section is reserved for the effects of acid precipitation.

A method for the joint statistical assessment of both water quality and water resources is currently under development in Norway. The related work started from the observation that general statements about water quality are often made on the basis of monitoring data, although such generalizations are not founded on statistical theory. In particular, monitoring data are generally not obtained from randomly located measurement sites.

The method aims at the elaboration of statistical procedures for the estimation of averages of water-quality parameters. The method involves the stratification of river stretches in order to arrive at generalized statements about water quality of water volumes on the basis of random sampling. The broader framework, within which the statements obtained appear most useful, can be described as a "water-resource setting" because the flow rate of water is used not only in the measurement of water resources but also in their quality assessment.

The results appearing so far from Norwegian methodological work have been tested for a Norwegian river basin and also briefly in the context of patrimony accounts. In both cases, the tests have been conclusive in the sense that they have yielded characteristic results in comparison to other methodological options. At the same time, the tests have highlighted a number of technical issues which could be resolved in further work currently under way in Norway.

POLAND

Statistical data on purity of rivers are collected in Poland by the State Inspectorate for Environmental Protection, on the basis of the results of river controls conducted in permanent measurement stations by regional units for surveying and management of the environment. On those rivers are located 1,280 permanent stations. In them the number of water samples varies from 4 to 12 within a year, depending on the degree of water pollution. The basic criterion of classification of waters is their suitability for various economic purposes (c.f. annex XI).

The network of section lines comprises all rivers with basins covering an area of more than 300 km^2, less if the economic importance at the national or regional level so requires. The classification of the state of cleanliness of the water is based on standards of permissible pollutant concentrations, determined by an act of the Council of Ministers. In the Statistical Yearbook relevant statistics on ambient water quality are published and compared with data from previous survey periods.

According to quality requirements, surface waters have been classified into three classes:

(a) First class includes all waters of a quality suitable for drinking water and domestic purposes, for industrial purposes where potable water quality is necessary for technological reasons and for fish-breeding of salmonidae;

(b) Second class includes water used for fish-breeding other than salmonidae, for animal husbandry and recreational purposes; and

(c) Third class covers waters for all other industrial uses, e.g. irrigation, horticulutre, greenhouses.

Some 60 threshold parameters characterize each class. They include general physical and inorganic and organic chemical, radiochemical and radiological microbiological, hydrobiological parameters as well as those of inorganic and organic industrial pollutants.

In recent years, due to the increase of pollution of surface waters, it has become necessary to define in a more precise way the binding methods for control and evaluation of the quality of flowing waters. Poland actively participates in those undertakings, inter alia, as a co-ordinator of research work on new and better methods of measurement and evaluation of water quality, conducted within the framework of CMEA. The present national system makes it possible to control the state and changes in pollution exclusively for surface waters. There are no statistics on the state of the quality of underground waters which constitute an important source of water for industry and for the population.

SPAIN

The General Department for Hydraulic Works assumes responsibility for surveying ambient water quality in Spain. Quality data are usually stored with data on water flow which are published annually for specific monitoring stations. The analysis of surface water is presented showing approximately 50 parameters including phosphates, nitrates, detergents, oil, phenols, cyanides and heavy metals. Spanish rivers are classified into three categories according to water use. Threshold values have been established for most of the above-mentioned parameters.

SWEDEN

A programme has been established for the supervision of environmental quality. Its objective is identification of long-term quality changes of water, air and soil under environmental stress. Another aim is to elucidate the ways in which different pollutants move within and between the various resources. The survey programme was expected to yield documentation which could serve as a basis for the elaboration of official quality statistics.

In the Swedish yearbooks of environmental statistics (first published in 1977) ambient water-quality data are included in the chapter on the state of the environment. Background information on ambient water is confined to natural characteristics of seawater and freshwater. This includes sea depths, salinity at surface, surface current, catchment areas of river basins, mean annual discharge at estuaries of principal rivers (measured in m^3/sec) and average annual run-off from river basins (measured in litres/sec/km^2).

The following variables are used as indicators of water quality: depth of visibility; suspended solids; pH-value; temperature (at various depths); oxygen; total phosphorus; total nitrogen; chlorophyll. Transport of suspended solids, organic substances, total phosphorus, total nitrogen, and total inorganic substances in rivers is shown by river station, together with mean annual run-off and catchment area above the river station. Data pertaining to the seawater surrounding Sweden relate to depth, salinity, oxygen content and temperature. Ground water is characterized by positive and negative ions measured, pH-value, tritium content, ground-water level, temperature and precipitation, all according to measurement station and geological characteristics of the exact sampling site.

With regard to classification of water quality, work has been initiated to get a general overview of the situation in Swedish waters for certain groups of substances. Such surveys have been published regarding eutrophic substances, organic compounds, heavy metals and other toxic substances.

SWITZERLAND

The Federal Office for the Protection of the Environment has been compiling and publishing ambient water-quality statistics. The most recent is the report on sewage purification and surface-water quality which gathered information collected by authorities at the cantonal level. Account was taken of the various water uses and their specific quality demands: for drinking water, chemical and bacteriological criteria are foremost; for fishing, it is important to have ample feeding animals present; and finally, for the sake of a sound environment, a rich population of fauna and flora is a basic condition.

For this broad assessment and for ease of comparison, mainly chemical parameters were used; furthermore a dense network for measuring chemical parameters already existed. It was also found easier to interpret statistical information based on chemical parameters than on biological ones which depend on a number of external conditions (hydraulic, geological, climatic, etc.). With four basic parameters — dissolved organic carbon (DOC), ammonium, orthophosphate and biochemical oxygen demand (BOD_5) — typical stresses on ambient water quality were characterized:

Categories	Orthophosphate mg/lP	Ammonium mg/l N	DOC mg/l C	BOD mg/l O$_2$
Unstressed	$<$ 0.03	$<$ 0.04	$<$ 1.3	$<$ 1.8
Low stress	0.03 - 0.1	0.04 - 0.15	1.3 - 2.0	1.8 - 3.0
Considerable stress	0.1 - 0	0.15 - 0.4	2.0 - 3.5	3.0 - 5.0
Heavy stress	$>$ 0.3	$>$ 0.4	$>$ 3.5	$>$ 5.0

In this context, it should be noted that comparison with criteria applied in other countries is only possible to a limited extent. Owing to the high degree of waste-water treatment, the relatively high dilution capacity of rivers in Switzerland and their high natural aeration capacity, almost no problems were encountered with oxygen concentration. The parameter of dissolved oxygen was therefore not taken into account in the assessment.

Orthophosphate was chosen as an indicator for pollution from human activities, as it can be directly assimilated by plants in their metabolism. Ammonium, both an indicator for communal and agricultural discharges, for point and non-point sources pollution, is a potential danger in water: (a) under elevated temperatures and alkaline conditions, it changes into ammoniak, a strong fish killer, (b) in aquifers it may lead to oxygen depletion and (c) it may form chloramine compounds during disinfection of drinking water. Dissolved organic carbon is an indicator for organic compounds including substances of a chemical and synthetic nature difficult to break down during waste-water treatment. Complementary, the biochemical oxygen demand represents organic substances which decompose readily. Nevertheless, based on the last two parameters, the natural background concentration must be taken into account.

A cartographic presentation had been chosen for the comprehensive display of results. It consists of a map showing surface-water quality according to one of the four parameters for each measuring site.

UKRAINIAN SSR

The hydrometeorological service is responsible for the State recording of water resources (except ground waters) and monitoring of their régime and quality. Recording is done through a network of hydrometeorological observatories, stations and posts belonging to the State Committee for Hydrometeorology and Environmental Monitoring, using various means to obtain information (artificial earth satellites, aerial, expeditionary and other methods of research on water bodies, in accordance with the forms, in the manner and within the time-limits specified by the State Committee).

The geological service is responsible for: recording ground waters, including the exploitable reserves, as well as for monitoring their régime and quality; and submitting consolidated ground-water data to the hydrometeorological service. State recording of ground waters and monitoring of their régime and quality are carried out in accordance with the forms, in the manner and within the time-limits specified by the Ministry of Geology in

agreement with the hydrometeorological service. It is based on information
obtained from ground-water exploration and a study of the water régime and
balance, using data derived from the hydrogeological work of other ministries
and departments.

UNION OF SOVIET SOCIALIST REPUBLICS

In the early 1960s, water conservation questions were raised to the rank
of national policy. During the next decade, special governmental decrees were
issued concerning pollution control in the basins of the Baltic, Azov, Black
and Caspian seas, and the Volga, Ural, Chu and Tom rivers, as well as the
Baikal and Sevan lakes. In 1981, a decree on protection of the Arctic Basin
waters against pollution was passed. This permitted extending the water
conservation strategy to practically every water body of the country. The
guidelines of this strategy are laid down in the Principles of Water
Legislation of the Union of Soviet Socialist Republics.

The USSR State Committee for Hydrometeorology and Environment Monitoring
assumes responsibility for information collection regarding ambient water
quality. Observation of the quality of surface waters is conducted on those
sections of water bodies which are exposed to domestic, industrial and
agricultural waste. Measurements are made with a frequency of a few to 12
samples a year of substances and conditions assumed to be present in surface
waters as a result of waste-water discharge: e.g. suspended matter, dissolved
oxygen, oxidizability, biochemical oxygen demand, elementary nitrogen,
phenols, petroleum products, synthetic surface-active agents and metal
compounds.

As with any other control system, control of water conservation calls for
organizing certain typical operations, such as gauging, registration,
analysis, decision-making and other pertinent actions. The former can be
arranged through supplying the control system with information, while good
decision-making and remedial actions can be ensured by integrated economic and
administrative leverage. Comprehensive information supply is ensured by two
information flows resulting from the annual analysis of water quality in the
Union of Soviet Socialist Republics and the national registration of water use
and conservation. A country-wide observation network has been set up to
obtain water-quality information concerning all national water bodies. All
water bodies fall into four classes, depending on their national economic
importance. Each class presupposes certain gauging frequency and determines
the number of gauging sites. These sites are located with reference to the
major water users of each water body. Such an arrangement of the observation
network makes it possible to determine, after appropriate statistical data
processing, the average condition of water in controlled water bodies
according to sanitary and fishery standards along with detection of pollution
sources.

Realization of the national water conservation strategy in the Union of
Soviet Socialist Republics - with the help of economic and social development
plans and a system of co-ordinated measures used by water inspection
authorities - has made it possible to attain radical improvement of water
quality in almost all watersheds of the country over a period of 16 years.

Under conditions of steady development of the country's productive forces, the pollution level has been reduced in many rivers, lakes and reservoirs. Improvement in water quality is shown by the rivers Ural, Kuban, Don, Ob, Irtysh, Belaya, Amudarya and Syrdarya. The efficiency of water conservation measures in the Volga Basin is another good example. The Moskva River, which is one of the Volga's tributaries, is being used for recreation and fisheries; it ranks among the cleanest metropolitan rivers.

UNITED KINGDOM

Water authorities in the United Kingdom regularly monitor discharges into rivers and the quality of water in the rivers. Occasional detailed surveys of river and canal quality have been published by the National Water Council, classifying the waters into four classes. The first survey of river pollution in England and Wales was organized by the former Ministry of Housing and Local Government in 1958. This was followed by surveys organized by the Deparment of the Environment in 1970 and 1975 with intermediate updating for the years 1971 and 1972. The results of the most recent national survey, the River Quality Survey of 1980, have been presented by the National Water Council.

The object of the surveys has been to classify tidal and non-tidal waters in England and Wales according to their degree of pollution. The method of classification underwent considerable revision for the 1980 survey. It is still under review, having been used for only one national survey, although water authorities make full use of it in the management of river systems.

The original classification was used for all surveys from 1958 to 1975. It was used again for most waters in 1980 in parallel with the revised classification. At the time of the 1975 survey, there was general agreement that the method of classification then in use should be replaced by a more objective one taking into account the potential uses of rivers. This led to the 1980 river-quality classification which is based largely on chemical criteria and has now been adopted by the water authorities in England and Wales. The decision to base the classification on quality criteria appropriate to potential uses of river waters has greatly reduced the subjective element in the definition of river classes and in their use in classifying any given stretch of a river. The change was thus from a general description of "pollution" of waters - in which a mixture of quantitative and qualitative measures placed arbitrary boundaries on classes according to the extent of pollution - to one in which the measures and class boundaries were determined by the quality of water required for various uses. The new classification is appropriate for non-tidal rivers, but has also been used in classifying canals. A separate classification has been developed for estuaries.

The estuary classification was adopted in the 1980 survey (some waters previously classified as "tidal rivers" were included in the "rivers" classification rather than under "estuaries"). Although the classification system for estuaries embraces the uses to which they might be put, the estuary quality classes are not directly related to use. Thus some subjective element remains in the choice of the point at which class A separates from Class B. This classification also differs from that of rivers and canals in the way in which a given stretch of water is allocated to a class. For rivers and canals, a range of mainly chemical criteria is specified. All of these must be met for the river to be included in that class. For estuaries, biological, aesthetic and chemical aspects are each given a number of points which are totalled to make a score; this score serves as the criterion for classification. There is thus a limited scope among the middle classifications to "trade off" a poor aesthetic score, for example, against a better biological score.

In addition to the chemical classification of river quality, the need was felt for a complementary classification based on biological factors, i.e. on the varieties of macro-invertebrates present at any site. Scores were calculated by listing the families of macro-invertebrates found, ascribing scores according to the values agreed, then totalling those scores. This classification is still in its validation phase and no groupings into classes have yet been considered. The results of the biological score system obtained in the 1980 survey were left as total scores associated with a very large number of specific points in rivers. They have been published in the NWC's "River Quality" as a map. Although there was a general tendency for the higher biological scores to be associated with waters in chemical class 1, there were sufficient exceptions to confirm the value of a biological classification in addition to the chemical classification.

The new classifications of water quality, particularly the classification of estuaries and the biological classification of rivers, having been used in only one survey, cannot yet be considered definitive. Different approaches have been sought for establishing classification systems for different purposes. The next survey, some time in the future, will provide an opportunity to compare the different approaches, to validate or develop them further and to start to use them in the measurement of trends.

UNITED STATES OF AMERICA

For the control of ambient water quality, as for any other programme to protect public health and the environment, there is a need for data and statistics to monitor accomplishments and to guide decisions on what the next step in a protection programme should be. On a national level, such information is obtained through the National Stream Quality Accounting Network (NASQAN) which consists of data-collection sites at the mouths of some 350 hydrologic "accounting units". The network is designed to provide a measure of the quantity and quality of water moving from one accounting unit to the next, and ultimately to the sea or across national borders. NASQAN data thus provide an overall measure of the quality of the country's major rivers.

A prerequisite to the design of NASQAN was an interagency project to subdivide the United States into hydrologic accounting units. For units with regular, well-integrated drainage, one station was placed as near to the downstream end of the unit as was practical. The goal was to measure and have access for sampling of at least 90 per cent of the streamflow moving from one unit to the next. However, because of parallel drainage patterns along coastal areas, and the complex hydrologic situation caused by dams and reservoirs, it was necessary to have more than one station in some of the accounting units. This water quality information, together with more extensive streamflow data, has been used to estimate the quality of the remainder of the outflows of a particular accounting unit.

Within the United States there is a growing practice to supplement data from fixed station networks with areal studies of water quality. Areal studies of rivers generally cover relatively short segments (usually less than 100 km). They are designed to define the character, interrelationships and apparent cause of existing river-quality problems.

COUNCIL FOR MUTUAL ECONOMIC ASSISTANCE (CMEA)

The leading water-management bodies of CMEA member countries developed in 1982 standardized criteria for the classification of water quality. Among other things, the criteria and principles for classifying the quality of surface water are spelled out. Two sets of criteria and principles were developed, one for running water and one for stagnant water.

There are two types of classification: from the ecological standpoint, and from the standpoint of suitability of the water for use. The first type of classification comprises the following classes:

Class I   - Very clean water;
Class II   - Clean water;
Class III   - Very slightly polluted water;
Class IV   - Slightly polluted water;
Class V   - Heavily polluted water;
Class VI   - Very polluted water.

Class VI in the CMEA system includes water the quality of which exceeds the standard indicators for Class V. The individual indicators and their numerical values by class are listed in Annex XII.

The second type of classification provides for three grades of water quality:

Grade I   - Suitable water;

Grade II   - Water whose use is permissible subject to suitable methods of treatment;

Grade III   - Unsuitable water.

Indicators and standards have been elaborated for four types of water use: drinking water supply, irrigation, pisciculture and animal husbandry needs. In the event of any one indicator in a given class failing to conform to the standard values, the water is disqualified and down-graded to the class below:

Pollution indicator	Class of water quality
Dissolved oxygen	III
Saturation in oxygen	III
BOD$_5$	V
Oxidability	IV
General classification	V

EUROPEAN ECONOMIC COMMUNITY

The Euroepan Economic Community (EEC) has been paying greater attention to matters of ambient quality: several directives, adopted by and enforced in member countries should provide a basis for the elaboration of water-quality sstatistics. As can be seen from relevant environmental protection legislation, water bodies and their quality are being considered from the viewpoint of use. The relevant directives together with their purpose and details are given in annex XIII.

ANNEX I

WATER-USE STATISTICS IN DENMARK

These statistics are collected, compiled and published by the Danish Association of Water Works. The statistical system is structured in three tables where data are specified for major water works according to the main elements of the headings given below.

Table 1: Production and water consumption

- Number of inhabitants in supply area;

- Amount of water abstracted by water works;

- Amount of water consumed by water works

    of which: supplied to others or received from other supplies

                 consumed in own supply area

                      of which metered;

- Amount of water used by household, by industry, by institutions and losses;

- 24-hour mean consumption and average specific consumption.

Table 2: Technical systems and energy consumption

- The character of aquifers;

- Number of wells;

- Maximum capacity regarding raw water abstraction and clean water supply;

- Water quantity actually supplied;

- Electric energy consumption;

- Expense for electricity and oil;

- Average price of total water supplied;

- Length of pipe system of raw water and of clean water pipes;

- Volume of reservoirs and the volume in proportion to 24 hours mean and to maximum consumption;

- Number of pressure zones, water meters and hydrants.

Table 3: Water treatment and water quality

- Type of water treatment (aeration, filtration, removal of methane, chlorination, etc. ...);

- Raw water quality (total and temporary hardness: pH and contents of $KMnO_4$, Fe, Mn, NH_4-N, aggressive CO_2, CH_4, H_2S);

- Quality of water supplied (total and temporary hardness: pH and contents of $KMnO_4$, total solids, Ca, Mg, Fe, Mn, NH_4-N, Cl, SO_4, NO_2-N, F and aggressive CO_2);

- Number of routine bacteriological examinations in raw water, in treated water and in supplied water.

ANNEX II

WATER-USE STATISTICS IN FINLAND

PART I

STATISTICS ON PUBLIC WATER SUPPLY, SEWER SYSTEMS AND WATER
QUALITY IN WATER UTILITIES

The following information is compiled by the Finnish National Board of
Waters (last year of reference: 1980):

- Distribution of water supply plants and sewer systems by size and by
  associations;

- Population served in general, in towns and in communities by public
  water supply plants, by sewerage systems and by water district;

- Distribution of water supply plants and sewer systems by categories
  according to population served in each water district;

- Number of water supply systems where average raw water or delivered
  water exceeds one or more given parameters;

- Water consumption in each public water supply plant per water district
  and per province;

- Distribution of water consumption per water district and per province;

- Population served and distribution of population served per sewerage
  system, and per purification method, broken down by water districts;

- Municipal sewer systems showing treatment methods;

- Waste water treatment works per water district;

- Pollution load over period 1973 to 1980;

- Crude sewage and final effluent load per drainage basin, and per water
  district;

- Organic matter and nutrients in crude sewage and final effluent per
  province;

- Material and length of water conduits and of sewers per water
  district, and per province;

- Building costs, operating costs and income of water supply plants and
  of sewerage systems per water district, and per province;

- Water charges and sewage fees per water district;

- Maximum values of analyses of drinking water samples;

- Water treatment methods and chemicals used in water supplies;

- Water quantities, source of abstraction and treatment methods per province, commune and intake;

- Analytical results specified by the most common 20 parameters for water intake, raw water, treated water and distributed water per province and commune.

PART II

INDUSTRIAL WATER STATISTICS

The following statistics, compiled by the Finnish National Board of Waters for the years 1977 and 1978, show the level of disaggregation applied for a detailed survey on water use and disposal in the industrial sector (figures in parentheses refer to the legend attached):

- Amount of water supplied to industries by source [classification: type of industry (1), source of water (2)];

- Amount of water used in industries by type and source [classification: source of water (2), type of use (3)];

- Amount of water distributed by industry and the number of plants distributing water [classification: type of industry (1): distribution to another enterprise, distribution to households];

- Amount of water used in industries for different purposes [classification: type of industry (1), type of use (3)];

- Amount of water metered at water intake [classification: source of water (2), type of metering (4)];

- Amount of industry's self-supplied purified water [classification: type of industry (1), type of treatment (5)];

- Industry's investments in reservoirs, flow regulation, water abstraction, water conduction, and monitoring [classification: type of industry (1), object of investment (6)];

- Industry's investments in water purification [classifiction: type of industry (1), type of treatment (7)];

- Industry's operation costs of reservoirs, flow regulation, water conduction, and monitoring [classification: type of industry (1), source of costs (6)];

- Industry's operation costs of water purification [classification: type of industry (1), type of treatment (5)];

- Annual costs of industrial water supply, and water charges [classification: type of industry (1), cooling water, process-and waste water, waste water from water treatment plant and power station, sanitary water, other water, rainwater];

- Specific waste water quantities (volume of waste water per product) in different branches of industry [classification: type of industry (1) - products of pulp and paper industry (8)];

- Daily per capita water use in social premises (sanitary water) in different branches of industry [classification: type of industry (1)];

- Amount of industrial effluents discharged from industry's own sewers per category of water resource [classification: type of industry (1); sea, lake, river, brook or ditch, soil (infiltration)];

- Amount of industrial effluents discharged into the municipal network [classification: type of industry (1); sanitary waste water, process waste water];

- Number of industrial plants connected to the municipal network and the number of industrial plants paying waste water charges [classification: type of industry (1); plants connected, plants paying effluent charges];

- Amount of industrial effluent metered [classification: type of industry (1); type of metering (4)];

- Sampling methods for pollution load analyses at industrial plants with monitoring obligation [classification: type of industry (1), automatic sampling in proportion to flow (I), automatic sampling independent of flow (II), manual sampling (III); water quality parameters (9)];

- Frequency of analysis (or other investigations) at industrial plants with monitoring obligation [classifiction: type of industry (1), continuous sampling, daily sampling, weekly sampling, monthly sampling, less frequent sampling, special investigation before 1978, other methods; water quality parameters (9)];

- Industrial pollution load discharged into water bodies [classification: type of industry (1); SS, BOD_7, P, N.];

- Industrial pollution load per river basin and sea area [classification: river basin or sea area; SS, BOD_7, P, N.];

- Pollution load caused by fish farming per river basin and sea area [classification: river basin or sea area; SS, BOD_7, P, N.];

- Oil, phenol and heavy metal loads reported by industry [classification: petrochemical industry, fertilizer industry, other chemical industry, mining industry, leather industry; oil, phenol, Fe, Cu, Ni, Zn, Cr, Pb, Cd, Hg, Mn, V, Ti, Co, As];

- Pulp and paper industry's specific loading from 1972 to 1978 [classification: type of product (8); suspended solids, BOD_7, phosphorus, nitrogen];

- Number of plants in different water districts with (A) and without (B) monitoring obligation [classification: type of industry (1); water district];

- Valid discharge permits as of 31 December 1978 (Fish farms in parentheses, although included in the preceding figure) [classification: water courts and NBW; degree of validity and preliminary notifications];

- Quantity of waste water treated [classification: type of industry (1); type of treatment (10)];

- Industry's investments in waste water disposal and monitoring [classification: type of industry (1); object of investment (12)];

- Industry's investments in various waste water treatment methods [classification: type of industry (1); type of treatment (13)];

- Industry's water pollution control investments from 1975 to 1978 at the price level of the year in question [classification: type of industry (1) (in plant measures, treatment plants and sewer systems), years 1975 to 1978];

- Operation costs related to industry's waste water disposal and monitoring [classification: type of industry (1); source of costs (12)];

- Annual and unit costs of waste water treatment plants [classification: type of industry (1); capital cost, operation cost, effluent charge, total annual cost, average treatment cost per cubic meter of waste water (own outfall, effluent charge)];

- Waste water charges and compensations paid from 1971 to 1978 [classification: years 1971 to 1978; water pollution abatement charges (to the National Board of Waters to the Ministry of Agriculture and Forestry), Fisheries indemnities (to professional fishermen, to owner of water area), other indemnities, compensation measures (fish planting, others)]

Legend:

(1) type of industry: pulp and paper industry, mechanical wood-processing, petrochemical industry, fertilizer industry, other chemical industry, quarrying, mining industry, metal production, metal-processing, textile industry, leather- and fur-processing, milk-processing, slaughtering and meat-processing, other continuous food-processing, seasonal food-processing, separate power plants, fish farms;

(2) source of water: aquifer, sea, lake, river, artificial reservoir, other industrial enterprise, municipal water works;

(3) type of use: cooling water, process water, wash water, water for social premises, other water, water distributed to other enterprises, water distributed to households;

(4)   type of metering: continuous metering, regular metering with fixed
      equipment, periodic metering with fixed equipment, periodic metering
      without, no direct metering;

(5)   type of treatment: disinfection, mechanical, alkalization, chemical,
      other plus aeration, ion exchange, chemical plus ion exchange, other or
      observation missing;

(6)   object of investment or source of costs: flow regulation, pipelines,
      pumping stations, monitoring, other own project, connection charge paid,
      connection charge levied;

(7)   type of treatment: mechanical, chemical, ion exchange, (chemical plus
      ion exchange), (mechanical plus aeration), other or missing data;

(8)   products of pulp and paper industry: sulfate pulp, sulfate pulp and
      paper, sulfite pulp, sulfite pulp and paper, dissolved pulp, fluting
      cardboard, wood paper, wood cardboard, wood-free paper, wood-free
      cardboard, fibreboard;

(9)   water quality parameters: suspended solids, BOD_7, COD, P, N, heavy
      metals, oil and phenol, pH, electrical conductivity, temperature;

(10) type of treatment: stabilization, neutralization, mechanical, chemical,
      lagoon, aerated lagoon, biological or combined biological-chemical, other;

(11) type of measure: reduction in water use, separation of different types
      of water fractions, change in process, renewal of equipment, production
      based on waste, evaporation and incineration, recovery, supervision and
      alarm systems, other;

(12) object of investment or source of cost: sewer, pumping stations, sludge
      treatment, effluent monitoring, monitoring in the recipient, other than
      own project, connection charge;

(13) type of treatment: unknown, stabilization, mechanical, neutralization
      chemical, lagoon, aerated lagoon, biological or combined
      biological-chemical, other.

ANNEX III

WATER-USE STATISTICS IN THE FEDERAL REPUBLIC OF GERMANY

These statistics are collected by the statistical offices of the Länder, then compiled and published by the Federal Statistical Office. The data are based on inquiries into (a) public water supply and waste water removal and (b) withdrawal and use of water in mining, manufacturing and thermal power plants for public energy supply.

A.   Statistics of water supply and waste-water removal

Data	Unit of observation	Regional breakdown
1. Statistics of public water supply; data are supplied by individual water supply enterprises		
Number of supplied and unsupplied communities and population	community	Länder river basins
Supplied population and kinds of water a/	community	Länder river basins
Volume and quality of raw water withdrawal by source a/	water procurement plant	Länder river basins
Volume and quality b/ of pure water withdrawal by source a/	water procurement plant	Länder river basins
Volume and quality b/ of processed water	water procurement plant	Länder river basins
Water withdrawal and water deliveries	supply establishment	Länder
Volume of water supplied by consumer groups (households, industry, others) delivered to other water works and water consumed by water works, losses	supply establishment	Länder

a/   Water withdrawal by source: ground water, springwater, rivers and streams, lakes or reservoirs; bank infiltration and ground water enriched by surface water.

b/   Water quality parameters: calcium ions; magnesium ions; total hardness; acid capacity; pH; electrical conductivity; chlorid ions; nitrate ions; sulphate ions; phosphorus; oxidizable matter ($KMnO_4$).

Data	Unit of observation	Regional breakdown
2. Statistics of public waste water removal; data are supplied by operators of sewage systems or of waste water treatment plants		
Number of communities and population served by public sewage systems and waste water treatment plants	community	Länder
Length of sewage system	community	Länder
Volume and pollution load c/ of untreated waste water and discharge into waters and subsoil	community	Länder river basins
Sewage treated in waste water treatment plants, communities and population served by kinds of treatment d/	waste water treatment plant	Länder river basins
Pollution load c/ of treated sewage by kinds of treatment d/	waste water treatment plant	Länder river basins
Efficiency (for specific parameters c/) of waste water treatment plants by kinds of treatment d/	waste water treatment plant	Länder river basins
Treatment and removal of sewage sludge by kinds of treatment plants d/	waste water treatment plant	Länder

c/   Waste water pollution parameters: suspended solids, chemical oxygen demand (COD), and biochemical oxygen demand (BOD).

d/   Kinds of waste water treatment: primary treatment (purely mechanical), secondary treatment (biological purification), and tertiary treatment (specialized processes).

B.   Statistics of withdrawal and use of water and waste water removal in mining, manufacturing industries (all tables divided into branch of industry according to ISIC divisions 2 to 4 */), unit of observation: individual plant, data supplied by enterprise; regional breakdown: rural district, river basin.

_____

*/   International Standard Industrial Classification of all economic activities (mining and quarrying; manufacturing; electricity, gas and water).

- Water withdrawal by source a/ and water received from public and other suppliers

- Volume of water inserted in plant and drawn off unused

- Volume of water used by single-, multiple- and circulation-use and types of usage (e.g. cooling water, production water)

- Volume of untreated waste water discharged into waters and subsoil by types of usage (e.g. cooling water, production water)

- Pollution load c/ of untreated waste water discharged into waters and subsoil

- Pollution load c/ of treated sewage and efficiency of waste water treatment plants by kinds of treatment d/

- Plants for treatment of cadmium-polluted sewage and its whereabout (regional breakdown by Länder)

- Whereabout of treated sewage

- Treatment and removal of sewage sludge by kinds of treatment plants d/

C. Statistics of withdrawal and use of water and waste water removal in thermal grower plants for public energy supply: unit of observation and data supplier: individual thermal power plant; regional breakdown: Länder, river basin.

- Water withdrawal by source a/ and water received from public and other suppliers

- Volume of water inserted in plant and drawn off unused

- Volume of water used by single-, multiple- and circulation-use and types of usage (e.g. cooling water)

- Volume of untreated waste water discharged into waters and subsoil by types of usage (e.g. cooling water)

ANNEX IV

WATER-USE STATISTICS IN HUNGARY

PART I

QUESTIONNAIRES USED IN THE DATA COLLECTION PROCESSS

THE NAME OF THE QUESTIONNAIRE	FREQUENCY	TOPIC a/	UNITS OF OBSERVATION	DATA SUPPLIERS
Statistical form for the activities of water works and sewerage according to settlements	annually	I,II	settlement	all water and sewer works enterprises
Statistical form for the activities of the water management enterprises (water supply, sewerage and baths)	annually	I,II	enterprise	all water and sewer works enterprises
Statistical form for the activities of baths	annually	I	bath	all enterprises functioning baths
Statistical form for industrial water use	annually	I,II	plant	industrial plants of the sample
Statistical form for the water supply of agriculture	monthly b/ annually	I	depends on sheets	district water authorities, water management enter- prises, association
Statistical form for production and services	quarterly	I,II	enterprise	all enterprises belonging to water management
Statistical form for the data on water resources management	annually	I	section of water- course	district water authorities
Statistical form for sewer network pollution	annually	II	county	water management enterprises
Statistical form for water pollution	annually	II	county, section of watercourse	district water authorities
Statistical form for water quality analyses	collection once in a year c/	III	water sample, sample point	district water authorities

a/   I Water use   b/ Some sheets are sent monthly.
     II Waste water discharge
    III Water quality   c/ Registration according to sampling.

PART II

STATISTICS ON WATER SUPPLY, SEWERAGE SYSTEMS
AND WATER QUALITY IN WATER UTILITIES

- Amount of water used by sectors of national economy;

- Average capacity and production of public waterworks annually for drinking water and industrial water;

- Summary data of water supply 1970 to 1981: drinking water produced, realized and supplied to households;

- Summary data of bath services 1970 to 1981: total number of baths (medical, sanitary, strand) and water use;

- Water production and water quantity sold by water management to the domestic, industrial and agricultural sectors;

- Quantity of drinking water and total water quantity bought by specific branches of national economy from water management;

- Own water production in each branch of national economy;

- Amount of water used for total industry annually (1965 to 1980) per source (own production, purchased, fresh and re-used water);

- Amount of water used by sub-branches of industry and sectors and per source (own production, purchased from public supply and elsewhere, fresh and re-used water);

- Amount of water for different uses in industry (process water, cooling water, boiler feed and rinsing water and its waste water discharge, non-productive purposes) annually (1965 to 1980);

- Purchased fresh water according to sub-branches of industry and sources;

- Fresh water use by sub-branches of industry and purposes (process, supplementary, sanitary water use, own productive use);

- Amount of water for different uses in industry (fresh water/re-used water) by sub-branches of industry;

- Balance of water use (fresh water, losses, consumed, discharged) of electric power production compared to other sub-branches of industry;

- Waste water discharge by sub-branches of industry and branches of national economy;

- Number of waste water emitters and waste water quantity discharged by sub-branches of industry, branches of national economy and towns;

- Capacity of waste water reservoirs, by sub-branches of industry and branches of national economy, 1975 to 1980;

- Quantity of (domestic, industrial agricultural) waste water to be treated and not to be treated; to be treated properly, partially, not yet treated; treated by mechanical, biological, chemical techniques;

- Amount of waste water treated (mechanical, biological, chemical) by sub-branches of industry and branches of national economy;

- Amount of discharged waste water 1975 to 1980 into rivers, standing water bodies, small watercourses, for irrigation, for other use;

- Water pollutants discharged from emitters (both domestic and industrial) regularly surveyed 1975 to 1980; 32 parameters including COD, TSS, oils, nutrients, phenols, heavy metals;

- Water pollutants discharged from emitters not regularly surveyed (1978 to 1980): 12 parameters including COD, oils, heavy metals;

- Quantity of discharged waste water for each district water authority, for catchment areas, and for water protection areas;

- Water pollutants discharged (COD, total dissolved substances, ammonium ion, total extractable substances) for each district and water authority, for catchment areas and for water protection areas;

- Quantity of industrial waste water and its disposal into public sewers, surface waters, soil, other, according to sub-branches of industry;

- Share of industrial waste water and domestic sewage in public sewerage systems annually 1970 to 1981;

- Waste water quantity discharged into public sewerage systems by various industrial sub-branches;

- Quantity of waste water disposed of into rivers according to catchment areas;

- Quantity of water use in agricultural sector (irrigation, fish farming, other) by water sources (own production, purchased);

- Irrigation capacity by territory and irrigation method in different years;

- Irrigation water quantity by type of cultivated land in different years;

- Composition of irrigated land annually;

- Utilization of water quantity by main supply work annually;

- Abstraction from different water sources for irrigation purposes per county;

- Quantity of water use in agricultural sector and production by each district water authority;

- Water production of agricultural main works by district water authorities and mode of conveyance (pumped or by gravity);

- Use of agricultural water (irrigation, fish farming, other uses, water quantity passed on, quantity utilized) produced by primary main works per district water authorities;

- Use of medicinal and mineral water according to chemical compound and temperature;

- Data on fines for waste water for every branch of national economy.

PART III

COLLECTION, STORAGE AND PROCESSING OF WATER USE DATA

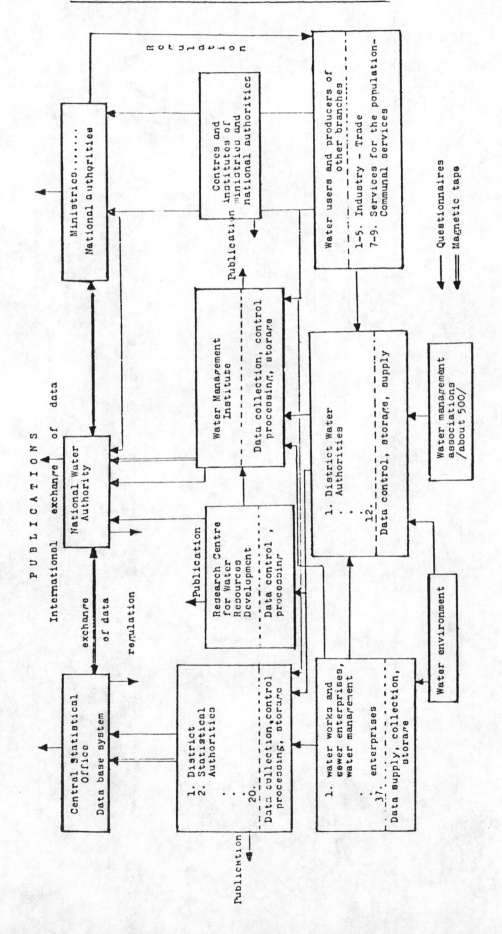

ANNEX V

WATER-USE STATISTICS IN POLAND

Since 1978, the most extensive work on water published annually by the Central Statistical Office has been the statistical yearbooks on environmental protection and water management. Apart from hydrographic data and ambient water quality statistics (most statistical information is further broken down by voivode) the data contain the following information:

- Water abstraction by resources and by sub-region: voivods, departments, hydrographic region (1970, 1975-1980);

- Water balance in industry and by industrial sector (1980);

- Enterprises using not less than 40,000 m^3 of water annually according to (a) the amount of water used, (b) surface and ground water abstraction and (c) water purchased of which from urban water works (1975, 1980);

- Enterprises using water for their own needs by volume of consumption (1980);

- Enterprises according to their equipment with closed water circuits, grouped by size of enterprise (1980);

- Mine waters in industrial enterprises (1975-1980);

- Piped water supply to households (1975-1980);

- Equipment of dwellings with water appliances (1970, 1978);

- Population and dwellings according to their equipment with water appliances;

- The convenience of equipping dwellings with water appliances;

- The water balance of urban piped water supplies (1975-1980);

- Towns and urban population according to their equipment with a piped-water supply (1980);

- Towns using public water supply systems, and consumption thereof (1980);

- Agricultural water supply, agricultural settlements and population, according to their equipment with water supply systems;

- Principle drainage or irrigation works and water drainage association (1975-1980);

- Area of drained or irrigated arable land, meadows and pastures (1975-1980);

- Water abstraction for irrigating agricultural or forest land and for filling fishponds, by irrigation method (1980);

- Irrigated agricultural or forest land, by irrigation method (1980);

- Construction of small water-retention facilities for agricultural needs (1976-1980);

- Area of pisciculture ponds (1980);

- Industrial and municipal effluent discharged to surface waters, of which requiring treatment, and by hydrographic region (1975-1980);

- Effects of treating industrial and municipal waste water (1980);

- Enterprises using not less than 40,000 m^3 of raw water annually and discharging effluent directly into surface waters, according to waste water requiring treatment and not treated; according to the water amount consumed (1975-1980);

- Treated and untreated effluent discharged by industrial enterprises according to voivode and industrial sector (1980);

- Treatment plant for municipal and industrial waste water by type and kind and according to the period of operation as well as capacity;

- Enterprises using not less than 40,000 m^3 raw water annually, according to their equipment with waste-water treatment plant; by type of pollutants discharged into surface waters; by number of workers employed in waste-water management, of which with a higher education (1975-1980);

- Towns and urban population as well as rural settlements and their population according to piped-water supply and drainage system; and equipped with sewage treatment plants (1970, 1975-1980);

- Waste water, of which treated and untreated, discharged to urban sewer network (1980);

- Characteristics of sewage treatment plants' equipment for mechanical and for biomechanical sewage treatment (1980);

- Water management and water protection investments (current prices), their material effects (1971-1980);

- Costs and material effects of water management and water protection regarding capital construction projects in municipalities; cost of these projects by voivode, by department (1975-1980);

- Capital investment and the material effects of a communal individual water supply to agriculture and villages (1975-1980);

- Investments and their material effects in the field of drainage and irrigation (1971-1980);

- Water management and water protection, capital construction projects brought into operation (1980);

- Water supply equipment brought into operation on individual farms (1980);

- Payments in respect of water consumption and effluent disposal (1978-1980);

- Utilization of water management assets (1978-1980);

- Flood losses (1971-1980);

ANNEX VI

STATISTICS OF WATER USE IN SWITZERLAND

I.   Summary of the contents of the publication "Statistical results of water services in Switzerland"

1.   Data collected and published annually:

   (a)   Water Supply:

      Private: spring water (gravity/pumped), groundwater and lake water;

      By regional networks: spring water, groundwater and lake water;

      By other services;

   (b)   Annual water supply:

      To households and small-scale artisanal enterprises, artisanal enterprises and industry, public services and fountains, water services, losses, supply to own network, supply to other services,

   (c)   Quantity supplied in 24 hours:

      Maximum, maximum per capita, minimum, minimum per capita, mean, mean per capita.

2.   Tables and graphs published annually:

   Development of mean and maximum daily per capita water consumption since 1945, water catchment in Switzerland (extrapolation), water supply in Switzerland (extrapolation), operating costs of water services in Switzerland (extrapolation), capital investment and subsidies of water services in Switzerland (extrapolation), personnel, synoptic table of extrapolated results, synoptic table of results for selected years.

3.   Data obtained annually, but not published separately:

   Cost of water, water monitoring (nitrates, chlorides, sulphates, pH, temporary hardness, total hardness), energy (consumption, cost).

4.   Additional data collected and published every five years:

   Water supply: pumping (number of pumping stations, installed capacity, quantity of water pumped);

Water disinfection: type of treatment, quantity of water treated, mean dosage;

Storage: number of reservoirs, total capacity of all reservoirs, fire-fighting reserve;

Water distribution: network (materials, length of conduits, maximum/minimum diameters); number of gates, hydrants (number, underground), pressures (maximum/minimum);

Water supply;

Metering and scale of charges: without meters (number of users, basis of the scale of charges) or with meters (system, number of users, cost per m^3;

Special users: number of properties supplied, number of public fountains, number of sprinkler installations, public swimming-pools (number, total capacity) and private swimming-pools (number, total capacity);

Water supply for refrigeration;

Specific data (in relation to the mean/maximum quantity of water supplied in 24 hours), installed water-supply capacity, reservoir capacity, length of network conduits.

5.   Additional tables and graphs published every five years:

Special survey carried out of alke-water treatment plants, evaluation of reservoir volume, energy consumption per m^3 of water.

II. Summary of contents of the statistical publication "The water requirements of Swiss industry"

By conducting a systematic survey of major Swiss enterprises using large quantities of water, it will be possible to ascertain the total water requirements of the following industries:

Gravel;

Food and fodder;

Textile;

Paper;

Rubber;

Chemicals;

Petroleum products, refineries;

Metallurgy and mechanical engineering;

Other branches.

The main criteria of the survey will concern the use of private sources and public sources; surface water and groundwater; supply costs; quantities of cooling water, boiler water, etc., the savings effected by in-plant measures; water consumption and water quality.

III. Summary of contents of the statistical publication "Treatment of waste water in Switzerland at the commune level" (1979)

Technical data on all waste-water treatment plants (classified in terms of (a) plants in operation, plants under construction and projects ready for execution; (b) number of inhabitants currently connected up in the drainage basin, (c) year of commissioning and extension of the plant; (d) technique applied in the mechanical and biological section, in advanced treatment and in the removal of sludges, including use in agriculture and discharge; (e) capacity of the station in terms of dry weather flow, number of inhabitants according to the project, hydraulic load, and BOD_5; (f) cost of the treatment plant without feed and discharge pipes;).

Proportion of inhabitants who can be connected up to commune waste-water treatment plants in relation to the total population of cantons;

Number of installations, number of communes connected, hydraulic capacity; construction costs by canton for plants in operation, plants under construction and ongoing projects;

Number of commune waste-water treatment plants in operation, classified according to capacity and advanced treatment;

Overall classification of waste-water treatment plants according to their characteristics;

Cost of constructing commune waste-water treatment plants in Switzerland between 1964 and 1978, according to their capacity;

Construction costs producing entitlement to a subsidy and the commitment by the Confederation in respect of waste-water and waste treatment plants, presented in tables as follows: (a) the whole of Switzerland for 1974, 1977 and 1978; (b) by canton for 1977 and 1978; (c) federal subisdies for the period 1960-1978;

Specific cost of operating mechanical/biological and mechanical/biological/chemical treatment plants according to capacity, planning costs, the cost of electricity and chemical products and sundry costs;

Quantity of waste water in total and central purification plants, according to capacity;

Total quantity of purification sludges produced in 1978;

Number of persons employed at each treatment plant, according to capacity;

Monitoring of sludge quality (heavy metals, etc.);

Number and capacity of commune treatment plants in operation, number of inhabitants, quantity of waste water and flows of water courses upstream in the drainage area;

Quantity of waste water in treatment plants in operation and by drainage area.

IV. Summary of contents of the statistical publication "Treatment of waste water and quality of surface water" (1983)

Technical data on all waste-water treatment plants (see chapter III);

Quantities of waste water and sludge;

Number of connections in relation to population;

Number of plants, number of communes connected, hydraulic capacity, construction costs by canton for plants in operation, plants under construction and ongoing projects;

Number of inhabitants within and outside areas served by sewerage systems.

ANNEX VII

WATER-USE STATISTICS IN THE USSR

Data on the following statistical components are being collected by the competent authorities in the USSR.

A. Water quantities and qualities per abstraction from natural resources (with indication on the distance from river mouth) or per each transfer from other enterprises water use for each month broken down by use (domestic, industrial, regular and irregular irrigation, agricultural use other than irrigation), and water quantities transferred to other users (a) without prior use, (b) after use and (c) losses due to water transportation.

B. Amount of waste water discharged per registration and per receiving water body (with indication on the distance between point of discharge and river mouth) broken down in (a) amounts with treatment or insufficiently purified and (b) amounts not needing treatment according to existing norms or waste water purified in treatment plants according to norms differentiated into biological, physico-chemical and mechanical treatment. Amount of fresh water metered, amount of waste water metered, amount of waste water discharged for filtration, storage or evaporation. For each entry and in compliance with details in the registration, the pollution load is specified including the following parameters: BOD, COD, total suspended solids, total dissolved solids, surface active substances, phenols, heavy metals, organic sulphur componds, H_2S, CS_2, aromatic hydrocarbons, chlorides and pesticides.

C. Indicators used to compare planning targets with actual data achieved in promoting rational use of water:

- Amount of water recycled in closed water circuits,

- Amount of water re-used in consecutive water-use systems,

- Number of filters in those systems used per year,

- Reduction of the release of polluted waste water in comparison with last year as a result of:

    (a) new purification plants or

    (b) improvement of technological processes and other measures,

- Total capacity of purification plants of which for biological, physico-chemical and mechanical treatment,

- Value of substances extracted from waste water including commercial oil products,

- Water use, total water abstraction.

ANNEX VIII

WATER-USE STATISTICS IN THE UNITED KINGDOM

The United Kingdom Department of the Enviornment compiles and publishes water use statistics according to the following structure:

- Annual abstraction by purpose (public water supply includes abstractions by water authorities, water companies and small private abstraction - spray irrigation and other agricultural use; central electricity generating and other industrial use) from surface water and ground water combined (1971 to 1981);

- Annual abstraction from surface water and ground water combined, by purpose (see above) for each water authority in England and Wales (1981);

- Percentage of abstractions for public water supply and of total abstractions from surface water, by water authority in England and Wales;

- Water use: water supplied, by water authority and by area (England and Wales, Scotland, Northern Ireland) and according to amounts metered and unmetered;

- Water authority expenditure on pollution control in England and Wales annually (1974-1982) broken down in revenue expenditure (comprises all running costs, interest, depreciation and, where charged to service revenue accounts, supplementary depreciation) and gross capital expenditure (i.e. expenditure on construction, provision or purchase of fixed assets or their replacement, improvement or major renewal, shown as the cost before deducting any capital grants or contributions receivable).

ANNEX IX

COMPILATION OF MAIN CHARACTERISTICS OF AMBIENT WATER QUALITY STATISTICS IN ECE COUNTRIES

ECE countries	Nature of statistical system		Classification into quality classes			Application of system		Use of statistics publications						Administration responsible for water quality statistics			
	resource oriented	use oriented	number of classes	approx. number of parameters	nature of parameters a/	ad-hoc surveys	regular	for internal administrative use only	partly for internal use	ad-hoc	regular (interval in year)	first public (year)	visual presentation of statistical data in maps	various administrations responsible	decentralized collection - centralized processing and use	centralized collection and use	automation
Austria	trophic saprobic	–	4		(b)	+	+		+	+			+	+		+	+
Belgium	–	+			(d)	+	–		+	+			+	+			+
Bulgaria	–	+	3	60	(e)			+									
Byelorussian SSR	–	+	4		(e)												
Canada	tests with stress				(e)								+	+	+		+
Czechoslovakia	+	+	5	25	(e)								+	+	+		
Denmark						+		+						+	+		
Finland	–	+	5	limited number	(e)	+					+		+				+
France	–	+	5	40	(e)	+			+		1	1971	+		+		+
German Democratic Republic	+	+	6		(c)+(d) (b)	+										+	+
Germany, Federal Republic of	trophic saprobic	–	4+3		(b)	+	–		+		+		+	+			+
Greece					(e)	+	+										
Hungary	tropic saprobic		6	50	(e)	+	+				+		+			+	+
Netherlands	+		5	3	(c)	+	+		+		1/4	1973	+	+			
Norway	+		4		(a)+(d)	+			+					+	+		
Poland	–	+	3	60	(e)	+		+	+						+		
Spain	–	+	3	50	(e)	+					1					+	
Sweden					(a)+(d)	+				+	+	1977					
Switzerland	–	+	3	4	(d)	+			+	+			+		+		
Ukrainian SSR						+		+								+	
USSR					(e)	+		+								+	
United Kingdom	–	+	4		(b)+(d)	+					4	1958					
USA						+			+					+			

a/ Abbreviations used to specify the nature of parameters:

(a) physical   (c) related to oxygen demand   (e) combination of all, including
(b) biological   (d) chemical   radiochemical, microbiological

Annex X

Quality classification for flowing waters in the Federal Republic of Germany

Quality grade	Degree of organic pollution	Saprobity (saprobic level)	Saprobic Index	Parameters a/		
				BOD5 (mg/l)	Ammonium (mg N/l)	Oxygen minima (mg/l)
1	No pollution or very low pollution	Oligosaprobic	1.0 - <1.5	1	At best traces	>8
1 - 2	Low pollution	Oligosaprobic with betamesosaprobic element	1.5 - <1.8	1 - 2	Around 0.1	>8
2	Moderate pollution	Betamesosaprobic	1.8 - <2.3	2 - 6	<0.3	>6
2 - 3	Critical pollution	Alpha-betameso-saprobic limit	2.3 - <2.7	5 - 10	<1	>4
3	Heavy pollution	Distinctly alpha-mesosaprobic	2.7 - <3.2	7 - 13	0.5 up to several mg N/l	>2
3 - 4	Very heavy pollution	Polysaprobic with alphamesosaprobic element	3.2 - <3.5	10 - 20	Several mg N/l	<2
4	Excessive pollution	Polysaprobic	3.5 - 4.0	>15	Several mg N/l	<2

a/ The data are reference values for frequently occurring concentrations.

Annex XI

Statistical Indicators for Ambient Water Quality
applied in statistical surveys in Poland

Specification	Unit of measurement	Frequency of collection	Level of aggregation	Source
1	2	3	4	5
Cleanness of rivers monitored, with measurements				Institute of Meteorology and Water Management
Total length of rivers	km			
Total length of monitored sections of rivers				
Rivers by water quality classes [campaign period] – general classification	km, %	Cyclical	Monitored rivers	State Inspectorate for Environmental Protection
First class				
Second class				
Third class				
Waters below standard				
Cleanness of lakes monitored, with measurements				
Total area of lakes	1 000 ha			
Total capacity of lakes				
Lakes by water quality classes	hm^3	Cyclical	Monitored lakes	State Inspectorate for Environmental Protection
First class				
Second class				
Third class				
Water below standard				

Annex XII

CMEA quality standards in respect of surface running water from the ecological standpoint

A. General physical indicators and indicators of inorganic substances

Indicators	Class of water quality					
	I	II	III	IV	V	VI
Temperature, °C	< 20	25	25	30	30	> 30
pH value	6.5-8.0	6.5-8.5	6.5-8.5	6.0-8.5	6.0-9.0	6.0-9.0
Dissolved oxygen, mg/l	> 8	6	5	4	2	< 2
Oxygen saturation, %	> 90	75	60	40	20	< 20
Specific electrical conductivity						
Micro Siemens per cm	< 400	700	1 100	1 300	1 600	> 1 600
Total quantity of dissolved solids, mg/l	< 300	500	800	1 000	1 200	> 1 200
Total quantity of suspended solids, mg/l 1/	< 20	30	50	100	200	> 200
Total hardness, H°	< 15	20	30	40	50	> 50
Chlorides, mg/l	< 50	150	200	300	500	> 500
Sulphates, mg/l	< 50	150	200	300	400	> 400
Iron (total quantity), mg/l	< 0.5	1	1	5	10	> 10
Magnesium (total quantity), mg/l	< 0.05	0.1	0.3	0.8	1.5	> 1.5
Ammonium N, mg/l	< 0.1	0.2	0.5	2.0	5.0	> 5.0
Nitrites N, mg/l	< 0.002	0.005	0.02	0.05	0.1	> 0.1
Nitrates N, mg/l	< 1	3	5	10	20	> 20
Phospahtes PO_4, mg/l	< 0.025	0.2	0.5	1.0	2.0	> 2.0
Total phosphorus PO_4, mg/l	0.05	0.4	1.0	2.0	3.0	> 3.0

1/ The values obtained in the event of a sharp change in water discharge should be excluded. The determination of suspended solids of natural origin calls for an individual approach.

B. <u>General indicators of organic substances</u>

Indicators	Class of water quality					
	I	II	III	IV	V	VI
Chemical oxygen (permanganate) demand, mg/O_2/l	< 5	10	20	30	40	> 40
Chemical oxygen (bichromate) demand, mg O_2/l	< 15	25	50	70	100	> 100
Biochemical oxygen demand (BOD_5), mg O_2/l	< 2	4	8	15	25	> 25
Organic carbon, mg/l	< 3	5	8	12	20	> 20
Extractable matter, mg/l 1/	< 0.2	0.5	1.0	3.0	5.0	> 5.0
Organic nitrogen, mg/l	< 0.5	1.0	2.0	5.0	10.0	> 10.0

1/ Extracted with the aid of carbon tetrachloride. Gravimetric measuring.

C. <u>Indicators of inorganic industrial pollutants</u>

Indicators	Class of water quality					
	I	II	III	IV	V	VI
Mercury, mcg/l	< 0.1	0.2	0.5	1	5	> 5
Cadmium, mcg/l	< 3	5	10	20	30	> 30
Lead, mcg/l	< 10	20	50	100	200	> 200
Arsenic, mcg/l	< 10	20	50	100	200	> 200
Copper, mcg/l	< 20	50	100	200	500	> 500
Chromium, mcg/l (total quantity)	< 20	50	100	200	500	> 500
Chromium (3+), mcg/l	< 20	100	200	500	1 000	> 1 000
Chromium (6+), mcg/l	0	20	20	50	100	> 100
Cobalt, mcg/l	< 10	20	50	100	500	> 500
Nickel, mcg/l	< 20	50	100	200	500	> 500
Zinc, mcg/l	< 0.2	1.0	2.0	5.0	10.0	> 10.0
Readily liberated cyanides, mg/l	0.0	0.0	< 0.05	0.1	0.2	> 0.2
Total quantity of cyanides, mg/l	0.0	0.0	< 0.5	1.0	2.0	> 2.0
Fluorides, mg/l	< 0.2	0.5	1.0	1.5	3.0	> 3.0
Free chlorine, mg/l	0.0	0.0	0.0	< 0.05	0.1	> 0.1
Sulphates, mg/l	0.0	0.0	0.00	< 0.01	0.02	> 0.02